Praise for *Revolutionary Woman*

"Get ready for a tall shot of whisky washed down with a warm glass of milk. You are lovingly kicked in the ass, wrapped up in a soft cuddly blanket and pushed out of the nest... all at the exact same time. It will empower the fuck out of you and inspire even the fiercest feminist into action. It's the book you didn't know you needed and every woman should read."

— Kristina Italic, Founder of
Evoke by Kristina

"This book is heat in your hands! So. Dang. Powerful. Get ready to walk tall, take up space, ask for what you need and receive it. *Revolutionary Woman* lights a fire in the soul and fans the flames with heart, humor, and healing. Shereen's writing feels like you have the most badass bestie/coach/mentor/mama right by your side cheering you on through the process of creating a life that is aligned with your desires. She turns the truth wayyyyy up and tells it like it is, so that you remember the Queen within and what you're here for. The words in these pages are for our mothers, daughters, nieces, girlfriends. Get this book for yourself and your loved ones."

— Christina Dunbar, Storyteller

"Consider this book your wakeup call — no, your rising up — to what's rightfully yours. YOUR LIFE. Your soul desires. Your goddamned female king-liness. With Shereen as your guide, you're in for the wonderfully rebellious, wickedly funny, heart expanding ride of a lifetime. So come on in. Join the Revolutionary Woman Circle. We've got you."

— Lisa Steadman, Bestselling Author
and Charismatic Creative

"This is a page-turner for Female Kings! If that line sparked you, hurry up and eat this book UP! Between the empowered humor and high truth baked into every word, you will be stopping to underline yet another truth bomb to come back to, post or share with your inner circle. This book doesn't simply give us permission...every word inside its rebel energy, page to page, reminds us that WE are the permission we have, at times, sought externally. Between her professional, life experience and high humor, Shereen Thor has written a must-read for any woman considering the next year or next 20 years of her life. Buckle up, buttercup and get ready for one regal ride!"

—MICHELLE GHILOTTI, Branding Strategist, featured in *ORIGIN Magazine* as one of the Nation's Top Creatives

"Powerful, witty, and will quickly help you unlock your soul's calling. This book should be required reading for all women everywhere."

— BONNIE FAHY, Founder of Source It! named the leading expert in outsourcing by *Forbes*

"Reading this book is an act of rebellion that will inevitably bring you closer to your happily ever after. By reading it and applying what's inside, you will save time, energy, and resources that are usually wasted on hiding your light, people-pleasing, and running from the truth. This book is a piece of Shereen, and it'll give you license to embody and manifest the revolutionary woman that you have inside."

— ROBERT MACK, Ivy League Educated Positive Psychology Expert and Celebrity Happiness Coach

REVOLUTIONARY
Woman

Break the Rules, Live Your Purpose,
and Find Your Happy

Shereen Thor

Revolutionary Woman

Copyright © 2021 by Shereen Thor

All rights reserved.

Except as permitted under the United States Copyright Act of 1976, no part of this publication may be reproduced or distributed in any form or by any means, or stored in a database or retrieval system, without the prior written permission of the publisher. If you would like to purchase bulk copies of *Revolutionary Woman*, please send your request to engage@shereenthor.com.

Printed in the United States of America.

Book design: Carla Green, Clarity Designworks

ISBN paperback: 978-1-7375394-0-7
ISBN ebook: 978-1-7375394-1-4

shereenthor.com

For my Maya

Your Free Gift

As a way of saying thanks for picking up this book, we're offering you our happiness cheatsheet. It includes the seven essential techniques that science says will increase your happiness now. To get yours, go to shereenthor.com/cheatsheet

CONTENTS

Foreword xi

Introduction xiii

1. Awaken the Rebel 1
2. Claim Your Kingship 23
3. Fuck the Joneses 37
4. Be the Truth 55
5. Ditch People Pleasing 75
6. Fight Like a Queen 99
7. Fuck Up Royally 119
8. Design Like a Boss 131
9. Be the Revolution 145

Endnotes 151

About the Author 157

FOREWORD

How many times have you pretended to be "cool" with something when in actuality, you're 100% NOT cool with it?

Once upon a time, in ye olden days, before I learned how to stand up for myself…

When my crush told me, "I'd love to come over tonight and see you, but you should know, I really don't 'do' relationships," I pretended to be fine with it because I wanted to be chill, sexy, un-demanding, and easy-going.

When my employer insisted that I attend five hundred million pointless meetings (all of which could have been summed up with an email), I went and politely took notes because I wanted to be perceived as a hard worker. I never complained even though the whole thing was wildly inefficient and inside, I wanted to scream.

When a male colleague (thirty years older than me) stopped by to "visit" my cubicle just to "chat" half a dozen times a day, interrupting me, and inviting me for drinks after work, I brushed it off and didn't make a fuss. Even though his constant intrusions made me feel profoundly uncomfortable.

When my boss noticed what was happening and asked, "is that guy bothering you?" I responded by saying, "um I guess kinda but not really." My voice trailed off into nothingness as I looked down at my keyboard.

I said, "not really."

What I wanted to say was, "hell yes, he sure is."

I bet you can remember at least one situation in your life when you pretended to be fine, cool, chill, unbothered, when inside your heart was breaking or your stomach felt like garbage.

Maybe you can remember a thousand situations like this. Maybe this sounds like your everyday life.

But now you're reading Shereen's book, Revolutionary Woman, which means you're ready for all that nonsense to change.

This book will encourage you to stand up for yourself, demand better treatment from others (and from yourself), and stop engaging in behaviors that erode your self-esteem. Sometimes, the simple act of saying "actually, I'm NOT cool with that" is revolutionary.

As Shereen writes, "You are a treasure." You are valuable beyond measure. If you've forgotten, this book will remind you.

With blunt advice, refreshingly honest stories, and a healthy smattering of curse words (hey, we're all grown-ups here right?) this book will get you riled up—in all the best ways.

What kind of revolution do you want to create in your life? Let it begin—here and now.

Alexandra Franzen
Author of *You're Going to Survive, So This Is the End: A Love Story,* and *The Checklist Book.* Co-Founder of Get It Done.
July 2021

INTRODUCTION

*A*s I sat down to write, I wondered if the title of this book would make me look like I had too much bravado.

Who do I think I am? Do I think I'm revolutionary? Who in the fuck am I to claim that about myself and invite other women to do so as well?

That voice inside my head (and yours) is the voice of the patriarchy.

Just as white supremacy has permeated us all regardless of skin color—we women have a strange, overbearing patriarchal inner voice that commands us to stay small.

I invite you to observe that voice. Acknowledge it, and revel in the fact that it's not actually *yours*. It's been taught to you. Handed down in the subtext of our culture, and unfortunately, it's been widely accepted—*until now*. After coaching for over a decade, what I know for sure is that what has been learned can be unlearned. That's what this book is about: the unlearning, shedding, and degrading of a trash paradigm. Followed, of course, by the proactive creation of a life that offers what we truly desire and deserve.

Who are we when we shed all the oppressive bullshit that we've inherited? What will we be like when we actually step into our innate power?

Those outdated paradigms were handed down by generations who did it wrong. Who missed the point. They done fucked up.

We need to "Forgive them for they know not what they do." But we also need to move forward powerfully as women. We need to overcome centuries of oppression and create a new normal that is worthy of us. We need to be revolutionary.

This book is not about blame; it's about progress. It's not your fault that things are this way, but it *is* your responsibility to move forward powerfully, and you've got this. Let's shed all that racist patriarchal bullshit and create a world we love to live in.

Don't worry, I know that the systems aren't set up in our favor. I know that the systemic oppression of women and people of color is real. But this doesn't preclude us from overcoming it regardless. The revolution must first happen within, and the world will transform.

It doesn't take much to be revolutionary. You can do it. You just gotta be willing to kick up some dust, raise some hell, and awaken the rebel inside.

So, if you get nothing else from this book, at the very least I hope you give yourself permission to misbehave.

1

AWAKEN the Rebel

Well-behaved women seldom make history.
—Laurel Thatcher

The mainstream self-help community loves to remind us of how much time we waste *not* following our dreams. We need to aggressively chase our passions with the tenacity of a tiger hunting its next meal, they say. We need to get so stinking rich through these passions, according to them, that we make money in our sleep. And, they tell us, we need to do all this whilst remembering that life is short and that the most important thing is to enjoy it with those we love. So, you know, don't be so busy pursuing your dreams that you miss your niece's fifth birthday party.

Don't get me wrong, I'm mostly onboard with their sentiment because I want those things for you, too, but I know that most women barely have time to pee in peace let alone define their higher calling.

They're staying up late mulling over a passive-aggressive comment from their mother-in-law. They're overloading their work schedule because the word *no* does not exist in their vocabulary. They're freaking out over the ticking time bomb that is their uterus while simultaneously wondering if they even want children. Or they can barely get through a single, uninterrupted thought because they're drowning in them.

Today's women are constantly juggling demanding work schedules, overbearing family members, codependent friends, social media appearances, and a multitude of other responsibilities. And despite all that we do for others, the heavy hand of societal expectations loves to make us feel like it's still not enough, even when we're working ourselves to death.

Our mothers and grandmothers modeled putting everyone else first, and it's expected of us as women. The patriarchy, which has been writing history for centuries, has been all too eager to cast women in the second-hand role of servant. All our lives, we're told to sit pretty, smile nice, and not make a fuss. And where has that gotten us? Stuck in lives where we feel suffocated and trapped.

Society says, "Be what *we want* you to be and you will be accepted. Be what *we think* you should be and you will belong." So we have become compliant at the cost of our souls.

One thing I always do when working with a new coaching client is help them understand how their actions affect them on an unconscious level. Sometimes they are living on autopilot and may not even realize that their choices are accidentally lowering their self-esteem.

If we had a real, honest conversation about what we are unconsciously saying to ourselves when we fulfill other people's expectations at our own expense, it would sound something like this:

> Thank you for allowing me to be a part of this group. I'm actually very unhappy fulfilling these requirements and meeting these expectations, but you are more important than me. I value your approval and respect more than I value and respect myself.

Don't feel judged, booboo, I am literally client zero. I've done this so many times in so many different scenarios, I'm expert enough to write this book.

I did it in college when I tried to dance like a fly girl at a frat party to look cool; dear Lord did I need to tone it down.

I did it at my first job when I tried to care about sports to fit in with all the white dudes who were in upper management.

And I did it when my man wanted me to play beach flag football with him. Don't get me wrong, I'm athletic . . . but I took it a little far because I was one month postpartum, so that shit was not cute.

So why do we do shit we don't actually want to do? Because, as humans, we're wired for connection. We need to feel seen, validated, and acknowledged for our contributions to the world. And science proves it. Recent studies show that the part of our brain associated with reward is more active when other people agree with or validate our opinions.[1] That hit of happiness is all we need to keep coming back seeking more and more social acceptance.

More often than not, it's easier to fill that need for belonging and acceptance by living according to other people's expectations rather than honoring who we were truly created to be, which might upset those people. I have many clients who do this to themselves every day. They have deep soul cravings that never get satiated. On the outside, their lives look great, but on the inside, they're starving for more. To write a book, to sing, to paint. They burn the candle at both ends meeting the expectations of work and relationships, but their own desires go unfulfilled.

Your desires are your map to your dharma. Your dharma is your true calling, what you were uniquely made for. However, many women are drowning in their need to please. So we abandon ourselves, and ditch our dharma in the process.

But just because we're feeding that natural impulse to belong by fitting in doesn't mean we are happy. As I'm sure you've experienced, ignoring your true desires in order to follow the conventional path may win you success on the outside—but it can cause total destruction on the inside.

When you're hustling to make sure nobody feels neglected, you often neglect yourself. This is the martyr archetype, the main socially constructed role for women that society accepts and celebrates. In 1914, women demanded a national holiday that was meant to be our very own declaration of independence. Woodrow Wilson did not support this, and instead he gave us Mother's Day to remind women of their primary role.[2]

For most of my life, I played the role of the martyr quite beautifully. Quite honestly, I'd been in training for this role my entire life. It made me a doting daughter, a supportive sister, a reliable friend, a thoughtful wife, and a loving mother.

You know what else it made me? Pretty fucking miserable.

If we take the fact that we are women out of the picture, which would inevitably remove all the societal constructs cast onto women, it begs the question: Is martyrdom a healthy way for a human being to live?

What Is a Revolutionary Woman?

A revolutionary woman is one who prioritizes her happiness and lives out her soul's true calling. This may sound like a tall order but all you need to do is be true to yourself and live authentically. If you do that, then living your soul's higher calling will inevitably happen.

Thanks to the patriarchal desire to keep women down, pretty much anything a woman does *for herself* is revolutionary. Honoring your true desires is a prerequisite to answering your higher calling. And answering your soul's higher calling is a prerequisite to happiness.

Using your extra cash to get your nails done simply because it makes you feel good. Quitting your soul-sucking job to honor your entrepreneurial spirit. Deciding not to follow the traditional path of getting married and having babies in favor of freedom and fun. Sleeping-in an extra hour because you're fucking exhausted.

Essentially, anything that men do without guilt or asking for permission is a revolutionary act when a woman does it. Kind of fucked up, isn't it? Being a revolutionary woman may sound like a tall order at first glance, but compared to the massive amount of oppression that women have faced over the course of history, it's actually pretty simple shit.

The biggest lie in life women have been told is that our purpose is solely to take care of others. Being a revolutionary woman means you honor your soul's higher calling, which sometimes ends up being viewed as selfish.

I'd like to discuss the word *selfish* because it's been used and overused against women for centuries to shame us into martyrdom. If your superpower is being a giving and caring woman, then it is also likely your kryptonite. Every weakness is just a strength overdone.

So, in this case selfishness is not a negative attribute—it is actually the medicine for that which ails you, which in this case is the disease of martyrdom. Selfishness will bring balance to your life, and for that reason it is part of your recovery from the addiction to other people's approval. This does not mean you need to be inconsiderate or rude; it's likely not even in your character to be that way. It just means you get to consider yourself along with everyone else rather than putting your needs on the back burner.

Systemic bullshit aside (and I know that's a LOT of bullshit), we must take the opportunities we currently have seriously. We must not squander them on lackluster living and passive existences where our sole purpose is to react to the needs of others. We must be the pilot of the plane of our lives, not the copilot.

You must take seriously this space you occupy on the planet—not because you don't deserve to be here but because you are here for a purpose. And although society would love for us to believe that we can pay attention to our purpose only after everyone else is taken care of, I am here to tell you that it's too important to wait until you can get a babysitter.

When you give up on your dreams (or pretend they don't exist), you're sacrificing your soul, your self-worth, and your dignity in exchange for societal acceptance. A lot of women do it—and it's killing us.

Studies have shown 120,000 preventable deaths a year can be attributed to stress.[3] Women are stressed not only because we're overworked and underappreciated but also because we're ignoring the work we've been called to do. My sage-ass best friend calls this soul sickness.

When you do work that is energizing to you—it *gives* you LIFE. When you choose to honor your soul's true calling, you don't burn out. You may get stressed at times, but you won't burn out, because the work itself is intrinsically rewarding. As you are outputting service, you're also giving yourself energy. It's a sustainable model for living. When we honor our dharma, we are rewarded with happiness.

When we work hard on something that drains our energy but doesn't repay us energetically—like when we sacrifice everything for our family or waste years at a job where we feel unappreciated—*our inner guidance system takes a beating.* It's like driving a car that has been needing gas for years but never gets filled up. This car—well on its way to a midlife crisis—is running on fumes and without a map to the next gas station.

However, if you're doing work and activities that are intrinsically rewarding, meaning, they fill your heart and light you up, then your gas tank gets filled as you work, and you stay energized and inspired, which creates longevity. You're living fully rather than killing yourself for societal validation or a paycheck.

Not only is the old model unsustainable, it's also tragic. Just imagine if J.Lo had decided that in order to make her parents proud she would become an accountant. Or if MLK had decided that his dream of becoming a preacher would never make him enough money, so he became an engineer instead.

I know this sounds hilarious and ridiculous, but we do this to ourselves every day. We decide to appease the herd for fear of being cast out of it. And we are literally DYING because of it. There is a term for this in Japanese relating to sudden occupational mortality: *karoshi*. It's literal meaning is "overwork death." The most common causes of *karoshi* deaths are heart attacks and strokes due to stress or starvation. Mental stress can also cause people to commit suicide. The phenomenon of death by overwork is common in other parts of Asia as well. This isn't widely discussed in every country, but our Western culture certainly celebrates hard work over well-being.

It's not just overworking that's killing us; it's also ignoring our dharma. By working yourself too hard on things that you aren't meant for, you're putting yourself at risk for a premature death and throwing away the gift of life.

Being on this nonstop treadmill and trying to convince everyone that you're okay when you're really not is a tragedy. We need to stop holding ourselves up to the societal measuring stick and wearing a lack of self-care as a badge of honor. We need to remember that we're human *beings*, and our worth is not based on how much we can do for others or how much we can care for others. Our value is inherent, it's not capable of being earned or lost. It's just a matter of fact.

If we were being honest about what the martyr archetype says to our unconscious mind, it would sound something like this:

I don't matter. Go ahead and use me as a puppet for whatever you need. It's okay if it slowly kills me. I know I am not worthy of being here anyway.

I see it every damn day when I talk to my amazingly successful, impressive, loving, smart, capable, and wonderful female clients. These beautiful women with hearts of gold, who make choices that kill them slowly every day.

They are queens living like servants.

Following your purpose is not selfish. You shouldn't feel guilty for those two a.m. moments when you face yourself in the mirror and admit that you want more than this. Not only is this okay, it's the truth. And honoring your truth is necessary for your survival and for the world to become a better place.

Just because our passive slow death has been normalized by society doesn't make it any less insane. We need to learn to listen to ourselves more than we listen to what others want for us. This is how we slowly but surely answer our higher calling and become fully self-actualized human beings. This is step one of healing from a broken system and becoming the revolutionary woman you were born to be.

Permission to Be a Rebel

As nice as it would be, you can't just snap your fingers and magically figure out your soul's purpose. To transform into the powerful, amazing force of nature you were born as, you must first give yourself permission to be guided by your inner voice rather than deferring your authority to others.

This also means that you must give yourself permission to sometimes look like an idiot, a failure, and a dumbass. Not because you actually are, but because people will judge you when you start to break out of the role they expect you to fulfill.

I first came alive in my life after attending my first personal growth seminar. We did all these closed-eyed exercises that I thought were cheesy and stupid, but they got me in touch with my wise unconscious mind and showed me how much I missed being who I truly am. I was quickly reminded of my essence and how long I had been pushing it to the sidelines in order to be accepted.

When I was a kid, I was energetic, bubbly, friendly, and alive. By the time I arrived at this seminar, I was twenty-five, working my first job out of college, and had already been sexually harassed. I was learning that I needed to be a "bitch" to gain respect in the corporate world, so it felt wise to toughen up to survive in that environment. Needless to say, that meant the bubbly part of my personality had to take a back seat.

After this seminar, I remembered who I truly was. I wasn't a bitch. I was friendly and warm. I was expressive and loving. I didn't want to go down the road of becoming someone else, even if refusing the widely accepted role meant I would look stupid or be perceived as a bimbo at work. So, I let my inner bubbly and big-hearted rebel take the lead.

I resolved to be the person I actually am rather than the person the toxic environment I worked in required. Instead of reacting to pain and allowing myself to become calloused, I would be a light in the world even if that meant it might hurt sometimes. I learned that pain and joy are two sides of the same coin, and if I wanted to feel joy, then I could not numb myself to pain. I had to be brave. I made the choice to be courageous and truly *live* rather than to stay small and slowly die.

I thank God for that cheesy-ass seminar every day because it changed the trajectory of my entire life. It woke me up and reunited me with who I truly am.

From that point forward I chose to honor my essence and hoped that in some way it would make the world a better place. I resolved to honor my authenticity instead of robbing myself and the world of whatever contribution I was uniquely meant to make. This is what I want for you, and this is the purpose of this book.

After the seminar, I quit a master's degree program I was only doing to gain my mother's approval and started doing stand-up comedy. This was a weird, and wildly risky, move to make, but it was the beginning of my journey from being a people-pleasing zombie to becoming a revolutionary woman.

It was a long road that led me to eventually finding my purpose, and the first step I took was halting my pattern of listening to everyone else over myself. My mom was so embarrassed of my comedic endeavors, she didn't want to tell her friends. She was part of a deeply dutiful religious community of Egyptians, and she didn't want me to bring shame to our family.

Knowing my mother was embarrassed of me stung. But I was done living for her. I was finally willing to be "bad" in order to choose my own path. And that's what I am inviting you to do.

The fact that you picked up this book tells me that you have some inner rebellious rumblings that desire your attention. Let go of what other people think of you. Let them judge you. How other people feel about you is *not* your problem.

You can be the black sheep. Give yourself permission to be yourself, and—let me be clear—only you have that power. The pages of this book won't change you. Only YOU have the power to change you. But the pages of this book are your official invitation.

I know it's scary to be perceived as bad, especially when we have been programmed to be good girls. We all have a deep desire to feel like we are accepted and like we belong. But in the words of our lovely Mother Teresa:

People are often unreasonable and self-centered; forgive them anyway. If you are kind people may accuse you of ulterior motives; be kind anyway. If you are successful you will win some false friends and some true enemies; succeed anyway. If you are honest people may cheat you; be honest anyway. What you spend years building, someone could destroy overnight; build anyway. If you find serenity and happiness they may be jealous; be happy anyway. The good you do today people will often forget tomorrow; do good anyway. Give the world the best you have and it may never be enough; give your best anyway. You see, in the final analysis it is between you and God; it was never between you and them anyway.

It's between you and your soul. You and your higher power. You and your higher calling. Your inability to be "bad" is often what keeps you falling in line, feeling accepted but unhappy inside. The part of you that wants more is likely what made you pick up this book, and I honor that part of you. You deserve more. You were meant for more, and I see you.

Albert Einstein said, "Everyone is a genius. But if you judge a fish by its ability to climb a tree, it will live its whole life believing that it is stupid."

You will never find the genius of the fish if you keep asking it to climb a tree. Who you are and what you're meant to do lies under layers and layers of clutter. Beliefs ingrained by society, your family, and the culture you grew up in.

You can talk about your childhood for eighteen hours with your therapist, but if you're still feeling blocked from reaching your purpose and potential, it's likely that you are unwilling to trust your intuition. Unwilling to bet on yourself.

Australian author and songwriter Bronnie Ware used to be a hospice nurse. She would sit at the bedside of those who were in their final days of this life, and she eventually wrote a book called *Top Five Regrets of the Dying*.[4] The number one regret is, "I wish I had the courage to live a life true to myself rather than the life other people expected of me."

Living an inauthentic life is a terribly painful experience, but in our society it's an epidemic—for which your commitment to changing your path is the only cure. Chasing your dreams and finding your truth are not selfish, first-world problems. They are the first of many revolutionary acts we must pull off to answer our soul's higher calling, unlock our purpose, and honor the women before us who fought so that we would have the right to do so.

So this is your official invitation to awaken the rebel. To live courageously and honor your soul's higher calling rather than die the slow death of deferring to other people's expectations.

Healing ourselves as women is the only way to heal our sick society. If you haven't noticed, good things happen when women lead. First we must learn how to lead ourselves. It's the only way to keep our communities happy, thriving, and alive.

If you're too much of a people pleaser to prioritize you for you, then consider doing this for our daughters. We do not want to pass the torch of oppression on to them. Let history NOT repeat itself.

The Systemic Disempowerment of Women

You are a woman. Although intuitively we know that can mean a vast array of beautiful things—from the soft, nurturing qualities we have to the fierceness we feel for those we love—we also know our gender's definition has been skewed, trampled, and violated for centuries. If I wanted to shorten this section into one, simple, all-encompassing sentence, it would be this:

We've been through some shit.

Paying even the slightest attention in your high school history class gave you insight into *some* of that shit, but I think it's important for women today to really know what our female ancestors went through. Those who fell asleep during history class (guilty) might wonder why knowing this information is important. And I'll tell you.

To be a revolutionary woman—one who makes the world a better place for the generations of women to follow—you have to know how we got here. How in the ever-living fuck did the world get like this?

Revolutionary women before us fought for progress so that we could have the opportunity to thrive. If we took the time to really understand the severity of what women have withstood throughout history, that fire under our asses might burn a bit brighter so that we can passionately pursue what we truly deserve.

I am shocked at how recently some of our basic rights were put into play. Even though we're now leading mass marches and calling out the disgusting actions of men in power, we still have a long way to go in terms of real equality.

So, let's look at some history that can help light that fire under our revolutionary asses.

1848: The Married Woman's Property Act passes in New York, which makes a woman not liable for her husband's debts and allows her to enter into contracts, collect rent, receive inheritance, and file a lawsuit without her husband's consent for the first time in the United States.[5]

Thanks for giving us basic rights, you fuckers.

1850s: Enslaved Black women—who were the most vulnerable group of Americans during the nineteenth century—started to be freed.

Thank God.

1908: Oregon limits women to working ten hours a day as a result of the fact that they are too fragile to work any longer and are needed at home.[6]

Most of what has held women back has been presented as "protection." I don't necessarily want to work more than ten hours per day, but I'd like to be able to make that choice for myself.

1920: The Nineteenth Amendment is ratified in the Constitution, allowing women to vote nationwide.[7]

So, let me get this straight. America was founded in 1776, and it took 144 years for you to realize this was bullshit?! Wow, you're quick.

1960: Women in the United States gain the right to open a bank account.[8]

Not very long before I was born—are you fucking kidding me?!

1967: Interracial marriage is legalized.

Oh, so I can marry who I love? Thanks for the permission, dickheads.

1963: The United States passes the first equal pay registration, but it's limited to a select number of jobs.[9]

Why, though?

1974: The United States passes the Equal Credit Opportunity Act, which allows single, divorced, or widowed women to sign a credit application—prior to this, they had to bring a man along to cosign for them.[10]

If it weren't for this one, my single mom would have had a really hard time getting away from my abusive father. No jokes here—just baffled this was so recent.

1976: Women in Ireland are FINALLY allowed to own their homes.[11]

1978: The United States passes the Pregnancy Discrimination Act. Until then, it was legal for women to be dismissed from their jobs because they were pregnant.[12]

What in the actual fuck. We forward the human race (you're welcome, by the way) and this was the thanks we got?! We do this massive essential service to humanity, and instead of being met with gratitude and reverence, we are met with "You're fired"? This is the perfect example of how sick our society has been.

1980: The Equal Employment Opportunity Commission defines sexual harassment.[13]

Took you long enough.

1981: The final law keeping women from owning property is overturned when courts rule that a husband is not allowed to unilaterally take out a second mortgage on a property he holds jointly with his wife.[14]

So recent—it's insane.

1993: The Family and Medical Leave Act finally becomes a law in the United States.[15]

Oh, you mean I get to actually stay home and spend time with this human being that I just ushered into this world instead of working for YOUR AGENDA every day of my life? Thanks so much . . . thanks so much for giving a flying fuck about what matters to me. Thanks so much for giving a flying fuck about what is actually in the best interest of humanity. Thank you so much for giving me permission.

Even though many of us were born at a time when things looked very equal in terms of laws, we're actually not as far along as we think we are. As you can see from that nifty and slightly disturbing timeline, it wasn't *that* long ago that women were living as second-class citizens. We needed permission from Daddy to open a bank account. We were treated like children and not allowed to do grown-up things.

Before we move on, It's important that you know that although I am pissed about what is unfair, I do not waste my time placing blame. It would be easy to point the finger at the racist patriarchy for architecting such an unfair world. And if I am totally honest, I did so for a minute (okay fine, maybe more than a minute) while writing this book.

But when you are being revolutionary, you don't follow your knee-jerk reactions. Placing blame is a typical behavior of the very racist patriarchal narrative I want us to move away from. So, I do not engage in such behaviors, nor will I encourage you to do so.

I believe we should raise hell politically in response to historical injustice, but we shouldn't wallow in the transgressions of the past. We can fight for systemic change and simultaneously choose not to wait fifty years for the government to create equality. We must revolt against the oppression that has been handed down to us with the knowing that the revolution first happens within.

The Reluctant Queen

This brings us to where we are now. Back then, our most obvious oppressions were physical and noticeable, but our modern-day obstacles are much more mental. This is where I come in. As a coach, I see what is visible as well as what is invisible.

Every day, I talk with women from all backgrounds, races, and income brackets who deal with the same nagging issue.

They feel *bad*.

They feel *guilty*.

And they feel like they are *not enough*.

They feel bad for not spending enough time with their partners. They feel guilty for not following the career path their parents laid out for them. They feel bad for following the career path their parents laid out for them but guilty for still feeling unhappy. They feel like they are not enough at work and at home because they are stretched too thin. They feel guilty for being a stay-at-home mom. They feel guilty for being a working mom. They feel bad for speaking up in a work meeting. They feel guilty for not speaking up when they knew they could have contributed. They feel bad for not wanting to have kids. They feel guilty for needing a break from their kids. They feel bad for spending money on a babysitter to have a minute of silence. They feel guilty for wanting alone time. They feel guilty for not being married. They feel guilty for wanting a divorce. They feel bad about their bodies. They feel guilty for living in a nice house. They feel bad for taking a vacation.

Guilty for wanting more—and guilty for having anything at all.

They just can't do anything right. No matter what path they take, they feel bad.

This isn't just what I'm hearing from clients, it shows up in the research as well. Statistically, women don't allow themselves to enjoy nearly as much of life's goodness as men do.

For instance, men will apply for a job when they meet 60 percent of the qualifications, whereas women will apply only if they meet 100 percent of them.[16]

What does this tell us? Men are willing to go after it, be ambitious, and take a chance on themselves because they trust in their abilities. But women hold back because they don't trust themselves to rise to the occasion.

Even if a woman gets that dream job, she will still be making 82 cents for every dollar earned by men, which is a gap of about 18 percent.[17] In fact, if change in pay equality continues at the same slow pace as till now, it won't be until 2059 that women receive equal pay to men. Fuck that. I believe we can speed up this timeline if we choose to step up and advocate for ourselves. We need an all-out revolt.

But what does it tell us? Our current society says that women are of lesser value than men even when they do the same exact job.

As disheartening as that reality is, it's even worse for women of color. Black women earn an average of 62 cents for every dollar earned by a white man. For Latinas it's 54 cents. For Native women it's 57 cents. Asian Americans and Pacific Islander women make an average of 90 cents, but some ethnic subgroups make as little as 50 cents.[18]

Holy shit, I can't.

And even when women step into their money-earning power and become the breadwinners of their families, they still do the majority of the housework—even when their husbands are unemployed.[19] Oh hell no.

Plus, we're all too familiar with the stereotypical idea that men manage and invest the money and women spend it. The research bears it out: About 58 percent of women leave all of the financial planning and decisions up to their husbands and male partners.[20]

So, legally we have rights we historically didn't have, professionally we have more power than we have had in the past, and yet we are still unwilling to wield that power to experience true equality.

The most telling statistic of them all is this one: Even in families where the woman is the breadwinner, 55 percent of women felt burdened by the role and only 35 percent felt appreciated for their contribution.[21]

I know this shit is in the ethers of our society, but as I write the information point-blank on this page, my heart can't help but break.

Even when we win, we feel bad for winning. Even when we are pulling tons of weight, we don't feel appreciated for it.

This is unfortunate. Statistics also show that men spend about 30 percent of their income on their families, but when women work, they invest about 90 percent of their income in their families and loved ones instead of spending it on themselves.[22]

So, when women win, EVERYONE WINS.

Get that in your head. When we win, everyone wins. We don't need to feel bad about it, or do more housework to prove we are worthy. We are magnificent. We are essential. We are queens. But, according to the research, we are queens living like servants. We are queens who are embarrassed of our crown. We're so uncomfortable with our power, we try to hide it.

All of those statistics boil down to a simple fact: Even though we seem to have all the same rights men have, we feel pretty shitty about it and give most of them away even though the world is better off with power in our hands.

Even though we can inherit wealth, own property, and open a damn bank account now, there's a dysfunctional amount of insecurity that shakes our confidence and holds us back from being as successful, happy, and empowered as we can be.

Collectively, we adopted an identity of disempowerment, financially and otherwise, which is why women are so often neglecting to take their full power in hand and wield it for the greater good.

You see, society has programmed men to achieve. They're told to take risks and go for it. They're told to feel good about their success. Women, on the other hand, we are told to accept whatever lot we're given and to be grateful we were given anything at all.

We are encouraged to do more with less, and look beautiful and ageless while doing it, to never complain, to keep that smile plastered on.

Although so many self-help books want us to believe that *we're* the problem, history shows that our current mindsets are just a by-product of the systemic disempowerment we've collectively experienced. It ain't your fault.

But now that you understand where it comes from (and what you're dealing with), it's time to take matters into your own hands and do the necessary mindset upgrades to finally accept your crown.

Whereas our ancestors had to dismantle old, oppressive systems, it's up to us to dismantle old, oppressive *beliefs*. I believe it is our holy duty to unlearn toxic paradigms and step back into the truth of who we are so that we can thrive in this life once again (yes, there was a time in history when women had more rights than we do in modern days; we will get to that in the next chapter).

When women win, everyone wins. So let's not be shamed into thinking otherwise.

How to Break Free

Now that you know the obstacles women have faced throughout history, you can see how *living your life for yourself instead of for someone else* is a revolutionary act. You can see that everything from owning your power to increasing your wealth to putting your phone on Do Not Disturb so you can get some rest is a revolutionary act.

One that you must live out in order to honor those who came before you, for yourself and for the women who will come after you.

I write this book with my daughter in mind. And I say to her, and to you, my dear, that these are the revolutionary acts that will support us in experiencing all of the freedom and dignity we deserve:

- Putting yourself first is a revolutionary act.
- Going after your dreams is a revolutionary act.
- Earning more (and more, and MORE) money is a revolutionary act.
- Loving your body is a revolutionary act.
- Trusting yourself is a revolutionary act.
- Establishing boundaries unapologetically is a revolutionary act.
- Honoring your ambition is a revolutionary act.
- Believing you are enough is a revolutionary act.

- Indulging yourself in what you love just because you love it is a revolutionary act.
- Celebrating your success is a revolutionary act.

Living your life on purpose and completely for you is a revolutionary fucking act. The women of history paved the way for you—and now it's your responsibility, a hard-won right you have, to thrive.

By picking up this book and doing this work, you're agreeing to something big. You will revolutionize your life, lead by example, and give other women permission to do the same. It's the racist patriarchy's worst nightmare.

And we're here for it.

— Life Work —

Let's awaken your rebel. Answer these questions in a journal and see what comes through. This exercise will support you in breaking the rules so that you can live your purpose and gain happiness.

1. If you gave yourself permission to "be bad" what would you do differently?
2. When you choose to be obedient, whose approval are you seeking?
3. If you break the rules now, what is possible for the rest of your life?
4. If you stay compliant, what will that cost you?

Fair warning—once you wake up your inner rebel, she'll never go back to sleep. Trust me, that's a good thing! We want you fully awake.

2
CLAIM
Your Kingship

I am, indeed, a king, because I know how to rule myself.
—Pietro Aretino

When it comes to power, women of the royal flavor have historically lacked it. The biggest names in female royals in our collective past—queens, princesses, first ladies, duchesses—held their titles dependent on having a male partner or guardian in higher power. The women who *did* rule sans husband were few and far between.

At least, that's what our public education system has led us to believe.

I don't know about you, but growing up I learned a lot more about white men than about anyone else. Besides Cleopatra and Queen Elizabeth, my knowledge of historically powerful women was about as vast as my knowledge of owl mating rituals. It wasn't until I was a curious adult who was in desperate need of some badass female role models that

I stumbled upon an especially seductive class of women who existed ages ago in ancient Egypt.

Female kings.

I'm a full-blooded Egyptian, so bringing you metaphorically back to my homeland might seem biased. But trust me when I say that you'll soon understand why ancient Egypt was the place to be if you were a woman.

Known by her subjects as queen regnant (BRB, adding *Queen Regnant* to my driver's license), a female king was a monarch whose rank was equivalent to that of a male king. And yet, modern society still can't get behind the idea of a female president. Go figure.

Unlike our traditional idea of queens (also called *queens consort* when they were married to a reigning king), who have zero power and are only there to birth the next—fingers crossed or you'll be beheaded—male heir, queens regnant had total sovereignty over their domain. They could start wars, end famines, create laws, secure partnerships, and throw total ragers in their castles.

In other words, these badass women were living the good life while making a massive difference in their queendoms—so, what happened?

As you now know from reading the last chapter, modern-day women's rights are still fresh-ass history that our mothers and grandmothers lived through. Even though back in the day we literally had the keys to the kingdom, the men of the world could not take a woman in power for long. Today, there are only two queens regnant in existence: Margrethe II of Denmark and Elizabeth II of the United Kingdom.

Although different kinds of female kings existed all over the world at different points throughout history, the female kings of ancient Egypt were true forces to be reckoned with. Which is a far cry from how the country operates today. My mother was born and raised in modern-day Egypt and was just as much a victim of the racist patriarchy as we are. She was told that light skin was superior and she was discouraged from learning to ride a bike for fear that it would make her "lose her virginity." You've gotta be fucking kidding me.

As awful as the current state of gender equality and female power may be in many countries, it's a sign of hope that there once was a time when both genders lived in harmony and equality. When both men and women could sit in the big chairs and make impactful decisions. It's my hope that learning this piece of *our* history will inspire you to fight for a future where we can experience that once again.

And unlike our last history lesson, this one will give you more hope, less rage, and you might even feel inspired. So let's dive in.

A World Ruled by Women

You've just stepped out of your time machine into ancient Egypt. It's around 2960 BCE, and Merneith is ruling—possibly as the earliest recorded queen regnant in history.[23]

She may have started her royal career as a queen consort to King Djet, but our girl Merneith went on to rule ancient Egypt after her husband died and before her son was old enough to reign. She was buried with all the extravagance of a Second Dynasty pharaoh. She was clearly the gateway drug, because this set into motion a long line of female pharaohs who were worshipped, respected, and valued for their leadership. Heck yes.

Back then, civilization honored the values of Ma'at, the Egyptian goddess of truth, harmony, and balance.[24] And because it was common for Egyptian religion to edify the feminine, women were highly respected and important members of the community even without a royal title.

Egyptologist Barbara Watterson writes in her book *Women in Ancient Egypt* about the freedom Egyptian women experienced during this time:

> In ancient Egypt a woman enjoyed the same rights under the law as a man. What her de jure [rightful entitlement] rights were depended upon her social class not her sex. All landed property descended in the female line, from mother to daughter, on the assumption, perhaps, that maternity is a matter of fact, paternity a matter of opinion. A woman was entitled to administer her own property and dispose of it as she wished. She could buy, sell, be a partner in legal contracts, be executor in wills and witness to legal documents, bring an action at court, and adopt children in her own name. An ancient Egyptian woman was legally *capax* [competent, capable]. In contrast, an ancient Greek woman was supervised by a *kyrios* [male guardian] and many Greek women who lived in Egypt during the Ptolemaic Period, observing Egyptian women acting without *kyrioi*, were encouraged to do so themselves. In short, an ancient Egyptian woman enjoyed greater social standing than many women of other societies, both ancient and modern.[25]

There's so much about this lifestyle that tickles me, but the "maternity is a matter of fact, paternity is a matter of opinion" part gets me excited. Finally some decency up in this bitch.

When I had my first baby, the feminist in me was born. Prior to that, I was pretty brainwashed by the patriarchal culture we live in: I valued my self-worth based on how much money I could make, how attractive I believed I was, and how much worldly success I had accumulated in the eyes of my peers.

But after popping out an entire human from my body, I was fully aware of (and totally awestruck by) the natural power women possess. In awe of the pain and suffering we endure to bring life into this world. In awe of the service to humanity we perform in doing what we do to forward the human race. In awe of how women intuitively know how to take care of each other and children in a way that men just don't.

And I was equally disturbed to realize that after going to literal hell and back, we're often oppressed by the men we create life with and the men we give life to. Once my eyes opened to *that* reality, there was no going back. Feminist Shereenie was born.

I finally saw how magnificent women truly are, and I couldn't fathom the oppression women endure every day any longer. If the world was a just and fair place (which it isn't), women would be revered and worshipped for our service to humanity—not oppressed. That's when my obsession with awakening the rebel evolved into an obsession with creating a more equitable world by empowering women.

But I digress. Back to ancient Egypt.

In addition to ruling and holding powerful roles in politics and society, women were also prominent in other ancient industries, such as medicine. Unlike other civilizations at that time, female doctors were respected and sought after. In fact, female students from other countries traveled to Alexandria in Egypt to attend medical school. Greek physician Agnodice was denied an education in Athens because of her sex, so she studied in Egypt and returned to Greece to practice disguised as a man—even though ancient Egypt had its act together, female oppression was still the norm around the world for most of our collective history.

Outside of the medical field, Egyptian women enjoyed success in other professions, too, such as "mistress of the house," which would be known today as an estate owner. They could also become scribes, seers, dentists, and priests and they could even run their own business.[26] That's right, boo—badass female entrepreneurs date back all the way to ancient Egypt!

When you compare the gender equality of this ancient civilization to that of our society even just two hundred years back, the difference is astounding.

A widow living in early-nineteenth-century America did not have any rights to home ownership. When her husband passed—or just skipped town for another gal, as they so often did back then—she had to depend on her male relatives' intervention to keep her home. When a woman living in ancient Egypt experienced the death of or legally divorced her husband, she could keep the home and run it as she saw fit.

It's crazy to think how far we have fallen from our rightful place in power—and how long it's taking us to get it back. But make no mistake. We are getting it back.

All Is Fair in Love and Gender Equality

Women were able to thrive in ancient Egypt because, in the eyes of the law, they were capable members of society. They didn't require any supervision and their plans did not require any approval by a man, nor did they need to consult a man in order to pursue any course of action. They were beautifully, blissfully free.

That freedom came with an awesome benefit many other women around the world did not enjoy at the time: freedom in love. Egyptian women could marry whomever they wanted—and divorce them whenever they wanted. Arranged marriages or being stuck in unhappy, dead-end relationships because of legal forces outside of their control was not a thing. These badass women were lucky enough to never feel the stigma attached to divorce that today's women feel. You know, the one that makes us feel like we can't leave a disrespectful, neglectful, and even abusive marriage.

I don't know about you, but I'd take equal rights over running water any day. The Nile River was pretty clean, right?

Even with the freedom to be single, many women preferred entering lifelong marriages because stable families led to stable communities. And it didn't hurt that prenuptial agreements were common and favored the woman. If a man decided to leave the marriage, he lost the right to sue for monetary gain and was required to pay alimony until she remarried or requested he stop. If the couple had any children, they would automatically go with the mother, and she would get the house unless he or his family had owned it prior to their marriage.

Speaking of children, women in ancient Egypt weren't viewed solely as babymakers in society. Married and unmarried women could get birth control and abortions if they chose to. Although virginity was often valued by men who desired marriage, whether a woman was actually a virgin on her wedding night was of no consequence. The only no-no in terms of sex at that time was extramarital affairs; women were discouraged from tempting married men, again because stable families created stable communities. This taboo was for the sake of the community at large, not used as a means to undervalue a sexually active woman.

Um—how close are we to building that time machine, again?

The Female Pharaoh

If that title alone doesn't give you goosebumps, I don't know what will.

Even though this past world was dominated mostly by male pharaohs, the first lady, or in their case the "principal wife," would occasionally take over and rule. This allowance gave birth to an entire line of female rulers who inevitably changed the course of Egypt's history. Let's learn their names—and bask in the beauty of female leadership.[27]

Prior to Queen Merneith (c. 3000 BCE), who, as you might recall, ruled as regent for her son, completely disregarding any patriarchal beliefs that only men could reign, came Neithhotep, who lived at the beginning of the First Dynasty around five thousand years ago. Neithhotep is the earliest known named royal woman of ancient Egypt. Her title inscribed in stone—"Foremost of Women"—may indicate that she ruled as queen. And her name is also positioned after the king's name, a spot usually reserved for the queen's.[28] They don't put this in the history books, but I'd argue she was one of the first revolutionary women to kick her society's outdated perceptions of women to the curb.

Then came Queen Khentkaus I, who wore the pharaonic beard and carried a scepter; next, Queen Khentkaus II, who was buried in a fancy tomb, indicating that she may have been a ruler; and then a few more queens regnant, who carried the ball and guided the kingdom till their sons were old enough to take over.[29]

Next came Sobekneferu, an amazing woman who ruled as king—not as queen or regent—from 1806 to 1802 BCE. She emphasized this point by attaching all five names for the king of Egypt to hers and adopting the male insignia to be sure she was recognized as pharaoh. She was buried with the full honors of a pharaoh, too.[30]

A few more powerful women contributed to the rule of ancient Egypt, acting as sounding boards and moral compasses to their husbands or sons, before Hatshepsut, fifth pharaoh of the Eighteenth Dynasty, came into power around 1478 BCE. She is the second historically confirmed female pharaoh (the first being Sobekneferu). Hatshepsut took it a step further by *having herself crowned* as pharaoh. She is still considered one of the most powerful and successful women of the ancient world, and she ruled for over twenty glorious years—longer than any other woman in an Egyptian dynasty.[31]

King Tut's grandma Tiye arrived on the scene in 1398 BCE and took hold of the reins of power during her long lifetime. Queen Tiye, wife of Amenhotep III, regularly took part in affairs of the state, acted as a diplomat, and even had her name written in a cartouche *like a boss-ass king*. If they sell cartouches on Etsy, I'm buying one for you ASAP.

After Tiye, Akhenaten's wife Nefertiti (c. 1370–1336 BCE) stepped up to the royal plate. At first, her role was family caretaker, but Akhenaten couldn't take the heat and abandoned his duties as pharaoh to concentrate on his new religion, so Nefertiti took over and ruled with grace.

The last queen to rule Egypt before it was taken over by Rome was Cleopatra VII (c. 69–30 BCE). She is among the best representatives of women's equality because she ruled the country far better than the males who preceded her.

Women's equality even extended to legends, one of which suggests that the god Osiris and the goddess Isis gave the world the gift of equality between men and women during their mythical rule. When you look at the high status, influence, and respect women commanded in this ancient civilization, you start to wonder if such a legend might be true.

Even though female pharaohs were in the minority, powerful queens were not. Throughout every nook and cranny of our diverse world, women undoubtedly exerted tremendous influence over their husbands, their court, and their country. However, this beautiful existence of women in power didn't last forever.

When Christianity began to rise in the fourth century CE, women became second-class citizens of the world. Thanks to the collective belief that Eve's "disobedience" was responsible for all sin, the female gender was deemed untrustworthy and of less value. Then, when Islam took over Egypt in the seventh century CE, the equality ancient Egyptian women had known for three thousand years ceased to exist.

So, there you have it: Women in Ancient Egypt had more rights than we experience today. As a woman embarking on revolutionizing the world for future generations, I believe ancient Egypt was our Eden—and we need to get her back.

Modern-Day Queens

I hope this chapter plants a seed in your mind of what equality could look like. I hope it sparks the idea that even though we've wrongfully endured centuries of submission, oppression, and abuse as a gender, we can get back to a place of power, peace, and control over our lives.

When I read about these ancient queens, I felt like a child meeting Mickey Mouse at Disney. Just as it doesn't matter that Mickey is really some sweaty dude in a costume, it doesn't matter that these women in power existed five thousand years ago. They're still a testament to what's possible.

Now, to be revolutionary you don't have to have a *Princess Diaries* moment like Anne Hathaway and discover you're the heir to some country you've never heard of. I want these women to inspire you to set the stage for you to rule the kingdom of your life on your terms.

Because it's about you. This whole book is about inspiring you to live a life you're proud of. And by doing that, you will, in all good conscience, change the world.

Our collective history is a prime example of how we become the stories we tell ourselves and that society reinforces. In an age when women were equal, we had no problem going after what we wanted, be it ruling a country or divorcing a shitty dude. And now—in an age when we're still coming out of the heavy fog of years of oppression—we can barely give ourselves permission to take a night off.

Although we have centuries of equality and power in our history, our experiences are a far cry from those times. Today, we're told to stay small. We're rewarded for being "super chill" and going with the flow, when the flow is someone else's idea. We're often made to feel like the only way we achieve success is to snag a man and have his babies.

No wonder it feels impossible to connect with our inner power. When a voice has been silenced for centuries, it has a little trouble speaking up. To help you turn up the volume on that voice, this book gives you guidance and exercises to reconnect with your authentic, intuitive inner power—aka your female king.

But before you get to that, I want you to try something a little crazy.

I want you to pretend to be a man.

Don't wear a fake mustache or start manspreading on the subway (okay, maybe do that last part), but I want you to close your eyes and put yourself in the shoes of a man. And not just any man: I want you to put yourself in the shoes of a king.

A powerful king spends his days ruling a country, being respected by his people, and indulging in his desires, whether they're important or seemingly frivolous. As a king, how would you react to some of the problems you have today?

If you really need a night off from ruling the world, and your partner let it slip that they made plans with their friends for the *third night in a row*, how would you respond?

If some asshole in a meeting presented an idea that was *definitely yours* in front of everybody, what would a king do?

If someone tried to tell you that you couldn't speak up, dress a certain way, or earn more money, how would Your Highness react?

For starters, they wouldn't let some commoner tell them that they couldn't wear their favorite sequin-covered cape to the ball. Fuck no.

Kings bow down to no one, and although that energy may feel foreign to you now, I want you to spend some time every day this week with it. Have some fun thinking about how you would live your life if you embodied the energy of a female king. I want you to focus on a stressful situation you're facing and tackle it like a king. Even if it's only in your mind or on a piece of paper.

Wear the damn crown and see what it's like to be that free. To trust yourself that much. And then, bit by bit, day by day, this energy will become less uncomfortable and more normal. Power is our birthright. Desire is our destiny. Women have been in the past and are currently here to rule.

And do you know what the best part is? You don't have to put on a man suit or wear expensive jewels on your head to get respect. The way people perceive you is a projection of how you perceive yourself, plain and simple. So, if you want to be respected, you must first respect yourself.

We have to give ourselves permission to rule ourselves if we are ever to truly rule the kingdom of our lives.

In this book, you're going to learn how to identify the blocks that prevent you from ruling your life as you see fit. Because when we don't feel worthy of what we want, we fight in a very disempowered way. Years ago, when I was arguing with my husband about money and equality in our marriage, I was screaming my head off because deep down I didn't feel like I deserved either. I was projecting my inner angst onto him, blaming him for our problems, but really I didn't believe myself worthy of money or equality to begin with.

When I slowly but surely evolved by harnessing my inner female king, I realized that I didn't need to scream to get what I wanted. I knew I deserved it, and because of that inner knowing, my husband responded very differently to my requests. True story.

We all deal with this. All of these ugly perceptions of unworthiness we have within ourselves are pushed out into the world without us even realizing that we are the cause. This is why mindset is everything, and why we're going to spend the first part of your revolutionary woman journey setting up your mind for success and dismantling these BS beliefs that only serve to hold us back.

After we do that, we're going to build up a vision of ourselves that's worthy of a female king. Because, baby girl, that's exactly what you are.

— Life Work —

Let's create your female king archetype right now. You can use this persona as inspiration when you're making the big changes required to be revolutionary.

1. If you were a female king, which one would you be? Nefertiti? Hatshepsut? Cleopatra? Choose the one that resonates with you the most. Have fun googling the shit out of her. Channel her energy this week and enjoy the freedom while claiming your kingship.

2. Each morning for the next week, choose one stressful situation you're facing. Sit with it for a few minutes and decide how a king would handle it. Write down your plan and go for it!

3. Journal on these questions:

    a. If I ruled my life like a king, what would I do differently?

    b. What mindset do I need to upgrade to give myself permission to live my life like this?

3
FUCK the Joneses

Happiness depends more on the inward disposition of mind than on outward circumstances.
—Benjamin Franklin

*H*appiness. It's a loaded word that can mean anything from sharing endless chips and salsa with your friends to fulfilling your dream of being a well-paid creative type.

And even though we know on a logical level that we can feel the emotion of happiness in the next twenty seconds if we want to, we overcomplicate it to a point where it feels out of reach.

I spent the majority of my life searching for happiness. Programmed to believe that it lived within the confines of white picket fences and respectable corporate careers, I dutifully went to college to become the quintessential cubicle monkey.

Nine-to-five job, mortgage, and Mom's approval in hand, I was understandably confused as fuck when the happiness I was chasing was nowhere to be found.

Sadly, my story of unsuccessfully chasing happiness is not rare. We think happiness comes in the form of partners and jobs. We expect to find it after we have kids and 401(k)s. And if we dip our toes in the pool of success, we are furious when we manifest everything we want and still don't feel happy.

So many people spend their entire lives trying to keep up with the Joneses. They put their true dreams and desires aside and waste their precious time trying to be the Kim Kardashian of their town. And even if they do make it to the level of success they think will make them happy, they still find that place can be empty and unfulfilling.

If you've fallen into the trap of this way of living, don't beat yourself up. It happens to all of us. Thanks to social media, it only takes a quick scroll on our phone to remind us that everyone in the world has a better life than we do.

Society has all but brainwashed us to believe that happiness is only accessible under the "right" circumstances. But the truth of the matter is that happiness is available to you right now. At this moment. Even if you're reading these words inside your shitty studio apartment or your childhood bedroom at your parents' house (we've all been there).

What I've learned from chasing (and ditching, and then refining) many life paths is this: Success will never make you happy. Achievements, goals, and glamorous material objects are good and fun to have, but they won't bring you any closer to feeling joyfully, authentically you—which is where true happiness lies.

So this chapter is all about helping you stop wasting your precious energy trying to keep up with the Joneses (whoever the eff they are) and start finding your happy.

The good news? The building blocks of happiness are all free, simple to do, and some only take a few seconds. The bad news? We've been so inundated by our toxic Western culture that we often see these simple steps and scoff. We're programmed to believe that nothing worth having comes easy, and thus, we complicate the simplicity of joy.

Simple joy. That's what you need to be tuning in to every day. If you want to chase after your dreams and run full speed into your ideal life, simple joy needs to be your baseline. Otherwise, you'll spend your entire life chasing after something that only leads you to something new to chase, constantly pushing happiness just out of reach.

Instead, when you operate from a place of love and appreciation for the life you've been given, everything flows. It's easier, better, and more fun. Your dreams take on a different energy, and you're so much more likely to fully enjoy everything you do achieve.

So let's dedicate this next chapter of our lives to rebelling against the idea that only the right circumstances create happiness. Let's unsubscribe from the drama and attachments to the possessions capitalism tells us we need. Let's prove to ourselves (and the world) that happiness and feeling good is a birthright you have access to *right fucking now*.

The Science of Happiness

I know you picked up this book to find your truth and live your purpose, but we first need to redesign our belief system as a prerequisite to supporting a new way of being.

Most of us have an "if-then" mentality when it comes to happiness. We think that *if* we become successful, *then* we get to be happy. *If* I get into that college, *then* I will be happy. *If* I get that job, *then* I will be happy. *If* I find my soulmate, *then* I will be happy, and the list goes on.

We defer our happiness into the future and tell ourselves we don't get to have it until we get "there." This is just a shitty trick our minds play on us, so don't fall for it.

But no wonder we do it! Our parents used to do it to us, too! "Eat your broccoli, *then* you get to have ice cream." It worked like a charm. And good for them because we needed to eat some fucking broccoli.

The problem is, we take that old-school parenting tactic and use it on ourselves. We continue to dangle the carrot of ice cream happiness far out into the future, so much so that we never actually get to enjoy it.

Spoiler alert: There is always a next destination on the road to "getting there." So, if you are deferring your happiness into the future, then the minute you attain a goal, you just defer it again. It's an endless cycle that just keeps you unhappy.

Let's kick that cycle to the curb, shall we? Not only can we see the evidence of its negative effects in our lives, but science recognizes it too. Research disproves this idea that "if we become successful, then we will be happy" altogether.[32]

This belief that success will make us happy is actually a lie, and the research suggests that it's the other way around. That's right—we got it backward, boo. In fact, it's happiness that actually leads to success. So, if you want to get your goals, first focus on increasing your happiness.

Happiness Myths

If you're shaking your head right now because you *know* that six-pack abs, a hot Italian man, and a Gucci bag *will* make you happy, allow me to drop some major truth bombs on you.

Let's start with money, the one thing many people would agree leads to happiness. We love to believe that most, if not all, of our problems directly result from a lack of money. If our bank accounts were flooded with cash, we'd be *much more* likely to wake up every day with a smile plastered on our face and hum show tunes while we stroll down the street, right?

Yes—but only to a certain point.

For sure, a lack of money can bring about a lot of stress, which of course impacts our ability to be happy. But a 2010 Princeton University study found that after a person reaches an income level of about $75,000 a year, their happiness doesn't increase.[33] That's the threshold where money stops having an effect on your emotional well-being.

The bills are paid, the kids can go to college, and you're no longer living paycheck to paycheck. But outside of relieving the stress of worrying about money, any additional funds don't lead to more happiness.

Next let's turn to another big one: material objects. We (especially Americans) love our things. From designer handbags to fancy skincare products and expensive cars, we tend to associate a level of happiness and success with accumulating higher-priced items. But again, science tells us that's far from the truth of how happiness works.

In fact, having a materialistic attitude can greatly contribute to your *unhappiness*. Research shows that even *thinking* about buying new stuff makes us less happy.[34] And when we earn the money and have the ability to buy all the worldly possessions that we desire, we're even more miserable.

Studies have found that materialistic people are not only less happy, but they're *more likely* to suffer from anxiety, depression, and substance abuse.[35] So, yeah—that new outfit you've been dreaming about doesn't seem so important now, does it?

On that same note, all the modern conveniences that we're used to, like Uber Eats and toilets, have no real impact on our level of happiness. A study found that people in the 1940s, a time when only two-thirds of homes had indoor plumbing and showers, rated their happiness levels as a 7.5 out of 10. In 2015, more than seventy years later and with access to everything we could possibly want or need in the palm of our hands, we rated our happiness as a 7.2.

If that doesn't prove that money and modern-day conveniences don't equate to happiness, then I don't know what does.

Okay, enough about our wallets. What about the other things society pressures us into thinking will make us happy, like a superhot body, for example.

I know I've fallen into this trap time and time again. It's reminds me of the meme that says, "Once I lose fifty pounds, clear up my skin, and get rid of my cellulite, it's over for you bitches."

Modern society and Instagram models love to tell us that losing weight is the key to happiness. But science tells us that it's not. Studies show that entering a weight loss program can make you more depressed.[36]

Now, for some people (not all), losing weight can be good for their physical health. But it's the stress of dieting and restricting your eating that can have negative effects on your mental health. That's why experts recommend slowly adopting a healthier lifestyle rather than trying to overhaul all of your eating and exercise habits at once.

My dad passed at the young age of fifty-six and I plan on living until I'm one hundred years old, so physical health is of paramount importance to me. I just make sure I am not becoming a statistic by beating myself up about it or choosing a program that makes me cry on the way to the gym (true story).

A probably less surprising scientific finding is that people who choose cosmetic surgery tend to be less happy to begin with, and they report even lower levels of happiness after the procedure is over.[37] Which might explain why this becomes an addiction for some. They keep chasing the happiness that they think is going to come, but it never comes, so they try and try again.

This is not meant to shame women who want to get procedures done; I have tried Botox myself—there's no shame in the beauty game. It's just meant to give you perspective on what we *think* will make us happy. It's meant to remind you that happiness is an inside game. If you know that and still want fuller lips, then feel free to go for it.

Remember this: Both the weight loss and plastic surgery industries are BILLION-dollar industries. So there's a lot of money to be made by making you feel bad about yourself and believe some surgery or diet pill is going to fix you.

The idea that we need to be "fixed" in the first place is more trash from the racist patriarchy, so don't buy in to it. You are a divine being, made perfectly in the eyes of your creator. No fixing needed whatsoever. Never forget that.

And, finally, let's reveal the truth behind the one thing EVERYONE believes will make us happier: true love.

Deep relationships and intimate connections are without a doubt crucial to living a full life. However, having a romantic partner, it turns out, doesn't make us *that* much happier.

One study found that when we do meet a special someone, we experience a spike in our happiness two years before marriage and two years after marriage. But once that honeymoon phase wears off, we return to the same happiness baseline we were before we met this person.[38]

So, deep relationships are not for nothing—you will get some happy chemicals in your brain for a bit. But having a relationship and being married are by no means the keys to long-term joy.

All of this goes to say that success (and all the things society has led us to believe will create success) doesn't lead to happiness. It's actually happiness that leads to success.

So there you have it, science has officially told you that eating ice cream is good for you. You're welcome.

As you can see, it's essential that we change our if-then mindset to a "right fucking NOW mindset." I get to be happy NOW as I go after that college, soulmate, job, Gucci bag, etcetera. I will not wait until I get it. I will experience happiness as I take each step toward my next destination.

This is true mastery: experiencing joy and contentment as we simultaneously aspire to more.

There is nothing wrong with wanting the things you want. You deserve to have an incredible partner, a closet full of designer clothes, a sexy bod, and a car so nice you're afraid to drink a latte in it. But you also deserve to believe and fully embody the fundamental truth that those things don't make or break you.

Beyond that, material objects and markers of success come to us so much more easily when we're not attaching all of our self-worth to them. When we let go of the idea that a boyfriend is the only thing that will make us happy and instead get happy right now, a boyfriend who we can be happy with comes into our lives much more easily. It's the law of the universe, and the sooner you start implementing it—the better (and more joyful) your life will be.

When You're Happy, Everyone Wins

As mentioned, happiness is more accessible than we think it is—we just have to give ourselves permission to feel it. We turn once again to the comfort of scientific proof to see that, if we build and commit to certain habits, then over time, we can make happiness our bitch.

Other than the obvious reasons why we want to be happy, tons of research proves that exhibiting positive emotions simply makes us better people.

A 2002 study published in *Psychological Science* found that happy people had more-fulfilling, high-quality relationships because they were less jealous and more agreeable.[39] A 2006 study published in the *Journal of Leadership and Organizational Studies* found that people who exhibited positive emotions regularly were less likely to miss work, and a 2002 study published in *Social Indicators Research* found that people who had a high sense of well-being were more likely to have a high salary.[40]

And a 2015 study found that unhappy people had a 14 percent higher risk of death than happy people.[41] So, just to recap, being happy will make you (1) a less jealous partner, (2) richer, and (3) less likely to die.

Seems like enough reasons to prioritize it daily, don't you think?

Lucky for everyone, being happy is not hard. Although we tend to believe that optimism and happiness are genetic and hard nuts to crack, we have more control than we think. Sonja Lyubomirsky writes in her book *The How of Happiness* that consistently feeling good feelings is actually a by-product of our actions, thoughts, and habits.[42] If we're constantly unhappy, it's probably because we've developed the habit of focusing on the wrong things, such as trying to control our circumstances or blaming our parents for our bad attitudes.

Being the positive psychology nerd I am, I've taken a lot of classes where I learned amazing and simple techniques that anyone can do *now* to feel happier.

Here they are:
- Utilize your strengths.
- Savor the moment.
- Practice gratitude.
- Foster connections.
- Perform random acts of kindness.
- Exercise.
- Sleep.
- Meditate.

When practiced regularly, all eight of these happiness hacks can help you feel positive emotions on a regular basis—which is necessary if you want to achieve your dreams, live your best life, and change the world.

Let's dive in.

Utilize Your Strengths

Nobody likes to feel like they're bad at something. In fact, recent research from Gallup proves that people who focus on their strengths (instead of throwing constant pity parties about their weaknesses) are three times more likely to report a high quality of life, achieve their goals, and experience less stress.[43]

Not sure what your strengths are? Don't worry. You can download my free Happiness Cheatsheet (go to shereenthor.com/cheatsheet). On the cheat sheet, you can find a link to a free strengths assessment and get this party started.

Research says that if you are using at least four out of your top seven strengths in your career, you are more likely to feel like it's a higher calling rather than just a job.

My top strength is humor, so it's no wonder I became a comedian and use humor in my podcast these days. My second strength is perspective, which I exercise regularly through coaching.

I have found ways to use my other strengths in my chosen line of work, and it makes all the difference. I feel happy, fulfilled, useful, and like I'm doing what I'm meant to be doing. I know that if you play to your strengths, too, then you will raise the level of happiness in your life.

Savor the Moment

Too often we let the best, most juicy moments in life whiz by without ever acknowledging them. Watching your partner read to your children, noticing your cat basking in the sunbeams coming in the window, watching your friends crack up at a joke—these are the things that make life great.

So how do we savor the moment? Slow the fuck down. We are so busy, too much to do, gotta do, do. Go go go. No, girl, you've got to soak it in. Yes, I'm hitting you with the cliché to "stop and smell the roses," literally.

We live in a culture that is obsessed with doing. But guess what, boo? You are a human BEING. You gots to take more time to BE.

We blaze through life unconsciously, and rob ourselves of the joy in each moment. Monumental achievements and accomplishments aren't what make us happy. The simple moments when we come alive inside build a life worth living.

We must consciously choose to sink into an experience by noticing the details and appreciating them. We must become more present in our lives. When I was taking a course at Yale called "The Science of Well-Being," the instructors had us practice savoring as one of our weekly exercises.

At first, I thought it was cheesy (just like that first seminar—are we seeing a pattern here?), but I figured I'd give it a try. One evening, my husband and I were singing a lullaby to my daughter, like we do every night at bedtime. I usually go through the motions, looking forward to the end because then I get some much needed downtime. However, I was told to savor, and for the first time in my entire life, it behooved me to do what I was told (just kidding! Not the first, maybe the second).

I looked at my husband and noticed how sweet it was for a father to sing to his daughter. How totally off-key he was, how singing wasn't his strong suit but he was doing it anyway—there was so much love in that moment. And to my cynical surprise, I STARTED TEARING UP!

What?! Holy shit, this savoring thing worked! One second ago, we were going through the motions, and the next I was so heart-warmed by an ordinary moment that I was in tears.

Research doesn't lie, boo. It's legit. Set a reminder in your phone to savor at least one moment a day and see if you can squeeze some more juice out of your already beautiful life.

Practice Gratitude

In addition to savoring life's little moments, practicing gratitude is another great, easy way to feel happy. Gratitude is like the Prom King of all happiness tactics. We have heard about it so often that we are kind of over it.

But let me remind you that gratitude isn't just a cliché. Research shows that regularly practicing gratitude can make you happier and healthier.[44] It can help you improve your sleep, recover faster from medical procedures, increase your energy levels, and even live longer.

I'd also like to note that social comparison is a happiness killer. When we see someone who has more than we do (or at least when it looks like it), our self-esteem decreases significantly.[45] And social media is like social comparison on steroids. So, if you want to think highly of yourself and be happy, get off social media or minimize how much you use it. A bit of wisdom, from me to you.

Gratitude is the antidote to social comparison. So start your gratitude practice by doing one of the following every day:

- When you wake up in the morning, write down five things you're grateful for in a gratitude journal.
- Start a gratitude note in your phone and use it at least once a day to capture things you appreciate.
- Right before you go to sleep, talk about the best moments of the day with your partner, kids, or pet or even yourself by using the voice recorder on your phone.

Have fun with it, but don't forget about gratitude. It's the good kind of Prom King.

Foster Connections

The quality of our lives is determined by the quality of our relationships—even the ones we have with our mail carriers and baristas. One study revealed that regularly participating in any form of positive social connection leads to more overall feelings of happiness.[46]

Typically, we interpret *social connections* to mean close friends or family. We don't want to be the weirdo on the bus or in the coffee shop making conversation with all the strangers. But strangely enough, research shows that we will feel significantly happier even if the social connection we are fostering is with a stranger.

We tend to think we are bothering people and don't wanna be "that guy." However, a little chitchat or positive affirmation for them or an expression of gratitude makes us happier and makes them happier. We all need social connection, in whatever form it comes. So, pick one positive social connection you can make or affirm every day and then set a reminder in your phone to do it. (You're going to have a lot of reminders set in your phone, so hopefully Siri has your back.)

Here are some ideas on how to foster connections:
- Listen to your partner describe their day after they get home from work.
- Read your children a bedtime story.
- Wave to your neighbor as you head out on your morning commute.
- Pop into your coworker's office for a chat.
- Call your parents to see if they've eaten any broccoli lately (joke's on them).

Perform Random Acts of Kindness

Remember how happiness can make you a better person? Well, a lot of that comes from the fact that helping and supporting other people is a surefire way for you to feel happy.

Whether you're picking up groceries for a grandparent, letting a stranger merge during traffic, or simply thanking someone for being a good friend, try to go out of your way once a week for another person. Not only will you be happier, but the world will be a better place.

Exercise

I know it's painfully obvious, but sitting on your couch or at your desk all day will actually make you miserable. If you want to experience all the benefits of being happy and following your dreams, you've gotta move that booty (oh yes I did).

Research suggests that thirty minutes a day of exercise can boost your mood in addition to making your body healthier. It's actually not about working out hard so much as it is about just moving more than you usually would. Try going for a walk after dinner or dancing around in the kitchen to your favorite song. Once you get comfortable with simple, daily exercise, you can bump it up to something more intense if you'd like. Whatever you do, just keep moving.

Sleep

Ever heard that saying "I'll sleep when I'm dead?" Pretty sure people feel really cool and fancy when they say it. Like they are superior to those lame asses who actually rest. I'm sorry to inform those maniacs that they need to calm down. Research suggests that sleep can improve your moods quite consistently.

Despite how obvious this is, so many of us fail to prioritize sleep. If you don't get a good night's sleep, you're more likely to be moody, quick-tempered, and emotional the next day.[47]

So take the steps below to increase your sleep hygiene so you'll be well rested and happier as you achieve your goals:
- Take the devices out of the bedroom.
- Don't drink caffeine after three p.m.

- Turn off the TV and your phone at least an hour before bed (maybe two if you're feeling like an overachiever).
- Develop a relaxing nighttime routine like taking a bath or reading a book.
- Aim for at least seven hours.

Meditate

There are so many juicy benefits of meditating daily, but gaining a more positive outlook on life is probably the best one. Much like exercise, you don't have to go crazy and meditate for twenty minutes two times a day. Just quiet the noise of life and give yourself five minutes.

I started a new practice of meditating regularly after the pandemic started in an effort to have a quarantine-friendly version of stress relief. It was in a meditation that the title and cover image of this book came to me.

When I started writing the content for Chapter 2 about the idea of being like the pharaonic queens of ancient Egypt, in meditation I started to see visions of an ancient Egyptian pharaoh depicted as a falcon-headed man. When I researched who this was, my vision closely resembled the image of Horus, the son of Isis, who represented kingship.

Depending on your level of "woo," this information I've shared might make you think I'm either a weirdo or a priestess. What I'd like you to take from these strange stories is that your unconscious mind harbors messages and gifts it would like to share with you to direct you on your path if you choose to tap in.

The research justifies the value of meditation by telling us it will relieve stress and boost our mood. But I am telling you that your connection to source lies inside of these quiet moments. The path to your purpose isn't "out there" on the internet or on social media or in the external world. It's inside you. If you quiet the noise, slow down, and go inward, you are more likely to find your path more quickly and easily.

You can try meditating in the quiet if you'd like, or you can listen to a guided meditation. You can even combine meditation with exercise or nature by doing walking meditations or sitting to meditate against a tree outside. There are tons of great options on YouTube as well as tons of apps you can download. I link to two of my favorites in my Happiness Cheatsheet, so feel free to enjoy those.

Just give meditation a try because it will change your life. It has definitely changed mine. It's given me so much confirmation about next steps and the right path. In my opinion, this happiness hack is not just a case for happiness; it's imperative to making sure you are honoring your inner voice, and living your life on purpose.

— Life Work —

Do these happiness habits every day for a week:

1. Utilize your strengths in your job or otherwise.
2. Savor the moment today; those roses smell good.
3. Practice gratitude by journaling five minutes every night about what you're grateful for.
4. Foster connections.
5. Perform random acts of kindness once a week.
6. Exercise every day for thirty minutes.
7. Sleep seven to nine hours a night.
8. Meditate.

Not only will you be happier NOW, but you'll also be in a much better headspace to revolutionize your life. I created a tool to make it easier for you to practice these habits in your daily life. Download my Happiness Cheatsheet here: shereenthor.com/cheatsheet.

4
BE
the Truth

A truth can walk naked, but a lie always needs to be dressed.
—Khalil Gibran

*I*f you picked up this book—or any book in the personal development aisle of Barnes & Noble, for that matter—chances are you've googled "how to find my purpose" once or twice.

There's no shame in your self-discovery game, but there is a lot of misinformation. Many of the books, seminars, and personal development programs out there promote this idea of finding your purpose. They market purpose like it's some multitiered video game, where moving up each level requires an erratic task like quitting your job, divorcing your partner, or paying tons of money to join an elite club.

But your purpose isn't something to find. It's something to be.

Many thought leaders and business coaches prey on the ego's susceptibility to social comparison to market their services and convince you that you need something outside of yourself to find yourself.

In reality, living your purpose and sharing your gifts are as easy as breathing. That's the energy we're looking to tune in to as we align ourselves with the person we already are and the life we are meant to lead.

The energy of purpose is the energy of ease. It's not made of the mind or ego, though your ego will certainly try to hijack the ride and take over. Purpose is a matter of the spirit. It's the energy of being versus doing. Allowing versus pushing. Flowing versus finding. It's less about making something happen and more about allowing the truth of you to come through.

If you're not into woo-woo thinking, relax. This isn't about spirituality or achieving some higher plane of consciousness. This is about allowing yourself to be who you've always been. You know, before society programmed you into thinking you should be something different.

In a sense, becoming your purpose is the process of self-actualization. But you don't have to go out into the world and achieve all these external things to find it. Rather, you must shed all of the layers of societal mind trash to reveal the core of who you are. Which is—surprise, surprise—your essence.

In my early twenties I made two major mistakes that took me off my soul's path:

- I followed my mother's definition of success rather than my own, and it was the wrong map.
- I veered off of the straight and narrow as a result of the pain I was experiencing in life and abandoned who I was by becoming calloused in order to "survive."

The first mistake resulted from a lack of engagement with my own heart in an effort to follow the rules, make my mom happy, and gain acceptance. In the end what it did was make me deeply unhappy and unfulfilled.

The second mistake resulted from me compromising my character in reaction to pain. We want to protect ourselves from pain; it's natural. What I learned (thankfully) on my path to course correction is that when you block your heart from pain, you also block it from joy.

Let's tackle the first mistake.

Why Do We Follow the Pack?

In my first big mistake, I pursued my mother's definition of success to try to make her happy with me, which is something a lot of my clients can relate to.

It doesn't matter if we're Beyoncé, Michelle Obama, or just a bored kid trying to break out of suburbia, our biological impulse is to appease whoever we believe to be in charge so that we can continue to be a part of the tribe. This isn't some woo-woo perspective on why we can't seem to leave our horrible jobs and chase after our dreams. This is science, sweetheart.

Belonging is one of the most deeply emotional motivators of what we do. So much so that way back in 1943 American psychologist Abraham Maslow listed achieving a sense of belonging as the third priority, just after physical and emotional safety, in his Hierarchy of Needs.[48] More recently, a study from the American Psychological Association determined that rejection and feeling no sense of belonging increase aggression and self-destructive acts and decrease self-control and intelligent thought.[49]

Wild, right? But it makes sense if you think about where we come from.

Being a part of a group and maintaining strong relationships (especially with your family) used to be the only way we could survive in a danger-riddled world. For thousands of years, being outcast or exiled from your community almost certainly meant death. Even though we're living in modern times, when independence and individuality are celebrated instead of punished, those old fears are still wired in our brains. No matter how much we act like we don't care, rejection from any of our social connections severely impacts us.

We felt it in high school when, out of nowhere, the friends we always sat with at lunch didn't make room for us at their table.

We felt it when we didn't get into that academic club or sorority because we didn't "meet the requirements."

We felt it when the person we thought we were going to be with forever broke our heart and married someone else.

Time heals all wounds—but it doesn't reprogram our brains.

When we stuff down the pain of that rejection and ignore its root cause, it infiltrates nearly every aspect of our lives. Being terrified of rejection and that form of isolation keeps us at jobs we hate and in relationships that hurt us. It prevents us from auditioning for that play or wearing what we want to. It pushes away anything and everything that might risk us feeling rejected. Why? We're wired to believe that being alone is worse than being unhappy.

But as you're discovering in this book, living in fear of rejection or of being cast out of the group is not only bad for your soul but also detrimental to your health. If you want to live a life on your terms—and you want that life to last a long time—you have to take responsibility for ridding yourself of old beliefs that don't serve your highest good. Then you can adopt new beliefs that do.

So give a big thank-you (and a middle finger) to the racist patriarchy for all the bullshit it's fed you. Commit yourself to unlearning that trash and choosing a life that works for you.

Pat your family on the back for deciding who and how you needed to be, and wave goodbye to that formerly forever-stuck version of you. Commit yourself to unlearning that paradigm and making your own decisions.

And, finally, say sayonara to the mainstream media for deciding what you need to look and act like. Commit yourself to unlearning that nonsense and expressing yourself in whichever way you choose.

It's time.

My Mother's (and Possibly Your Parent's) Definition of Success

As the daughter of an immigrant, I was expected to become a doctor, a lawyer, or an engineer. If you didn't already know, immigrant families offer only one type of love: the conditional kind.

But I did not fit the mold my mother had crafted for me. I was a creative type, a wild child, and a free spirit. So I was caught between two choices:

1. Pursue one of the aforementioned acceptable careers while acting deeply dutiful and religious so I could get married and make babies.
2. Walk to the beat of my own drum and forever be rejected by the only family I ever had.

Because I desperately wanted to feel like I belonged in my family, gain love and acceptance from my mother, and be seen as acceptable in the eyes of the community, I chose compliance.

Even though societal rules grated against my soul, I was terrified of disappointing everyone I loved. So much so that it kept me from doing anything remarkable for many years. Like many people, I chose to live in an inauthentic way that went against my nature so I wouldn't get kicked out of the pack.

And it took a lot of deep dissatisfaction with my lukewarm living to get me back on the right path. As someone who has spent a lot of time wishing she could live life a certain way, but never doing anything about it, trust me when I say: Spend as little time in this stage of your life as possible. Your dissatisfaction is a message from your soul, and it will NOT go away until you address it.

Your soul is a bad bitch, and she has your back.

Life Purpose Life Work

The only reason we ever shove down our deepest desires and impulses is because we are in survival mode. Back in the day, surviving meant remaining with our pack and having access to food, water, shelter, and the safety of the group. Now, surviving means having access to the kind of social connections and opportunities we think will make us happy (i.e., running with the popular crowd to get invited to cool parties, or any other form of social games we play to feel worthy).

Although the intensity of the urge to belong is the same, it's no longer a matter of life and death. But nobody bothered to tell our brains that.

When we attempt to do life through the lens of surviving, we're not only hurting ourselves. We're hurting other people too. Those closest to us are the ones who suffer from our apathy, our dissatisfaction, and our lack of enthusiasm for life. But if we attempted to thrive, not only individually but together as a family, as a community, as a society, then the world would be a much more beautiful place.

So, if you're game for changing yourself *and* the world, I'd like to invite you to thrive by taking the first step—creating your own definition of success by crafting your very own Life Purpose Statement.

I can't create this for you; it must come from you. Even if you are confused about what you want—many of us block ourselves from hearing our truth by telling ourselves we are confused—I'd like to assure you that no one is better equipped to hear you than you. Allow your emotions and energy to serve as your inner compass, guiding you to what you want. And if you're feeling really wild, you can even meditate to tune in to your inner voice.

Don't waste your time being scared right now. Just resolve to be disgustingly honest for the next few moments and write down whatever comes. This is between you and you, no one else. So I want you to quiet the noise in your mind and write down in a journal what comes to your heart when you ask the following questions:

- What does my ideal life look like?
- What does my soul truly want?
- If I died today, what would I regret not having done?
- What is truly important to me?
- If I had no fear, what would I create?

After you've spent some time meditating on this, I want you to use your answers to craft your Life Purpose Statement. To give you a little inspiration, here is mine:

> I want to empower women to unapologetically be who they are and answer their soul's higher calling.

Now, before you start trying to brainstorm "how" you'll turn your life purpose into a career that will make you millions and get you verified on Instagram, let me dissect what my Life Purpose Statement *really* means.

Empowering women isn't what I do for a living. It's not my job title. It's not what I put on my résumé. It's not attached to how many clients I have or how much money I'm making. In fact, it's not determined or influenced by anything external. It's just who I am.

Yes, I've crafted a business that *allows* me to empower women for a living, but I can just as easily empower a woman while standing in line at the grocery store as I can on a coach call. I don't need any fancy equipment to live my life purpose, and I can do it anywhere. No matter what is going on in my life, I can always make a point to empower women.

And because I know this deep down in my soul, I'm never lost. I may feel lost at times, which is the plight of creative types, but I'm never actually lost.

The reason you write down your Life Purpose Statement isn't to call in some big dream or manifest a new job opportunity. It's actually quite the opposite. A Life Purpose Statement is meant to anchor you throughout your life. It's there to remind you of who you really are no matter where you are or what you're doing.

Now that you've got the gist of what a Life Purpose Statement is meant to do, write yours down. Don't overthink it, just take a deep breath and write whatever comes.

As you can see, we were never lost. We've just been looking in the wrong direction. We've been trying to find some external solution to fix an internal problem that was never really broken in the first place.

So you don't have to move across the country or meditate on a mountaintop for ten days straight to find your purpose. You can if you want to, but you don't need to. But what do you have to do?

Be Who You Truly Are

Living your life purpose is the same as being true to who you are. Now that you've peeled back all the layers of BS and revealed your core desire for being on this planet, it's time to put all that juicy clarity into practice.

Although I talked a lot about how your purpose is supposed to feel like ease and flow, it won't in the beginning. You'll most likely be going against everything you've ever felt was "right" in this world. You'll be venturing into the unknown—and ruffling a lot of feathers in the process.

It will feel like you're trying to "make" something happen. And that's okay.

Even though you might think you have your purpose narrowed down, chances are, you will revamp, remold, and redo your Life Purpose

Statement a few times while you put it into practice. Don't let yourself get discouraged by the experimentation of it all. Embrace the mess and have fun with it. This is truly what life is all about, it's a creative process. This is a moment when you get to choose to *enjoy* the experience of discovering your life purpose rather than making it a miserable exercise. Suffering is definitely optional.

Don't forget, every moment is a choice for you to decide how and who you want to be. Do you want the process of self-actualization to be disconcerting and confusing? Or do you want it to be fun and freeing? You get to choose—but please choose wisely. You are the pilot of your plane, so how do you want to steer your flight?

Intrinsic and Extrinsic Expressions

When it comes to living your purpose, it turns out there are two routes to take: intrinsic and extrinsic.

Intrinsic motivation is when you do something simply because the act itself is personally rewarding. You sing in your church choir because it brings you joy, not because you want to be famous. Nobody may ever know that you care as much as you do about doing this thing—and you might not even know *why* you care so much—but you do. And that's more than enough of a reason to honor the impulse.

Extrinsic motivation, on the other hand, is when you do something because you'll be rewarded for doing it or punished for failing to fulfill a set expectation. Think of extrinsic motivation as the carrot *and* the stick—you act as the mule driver expects, and you may get the carrot, but if not, then the stick. Something outside of yourself is "encouraging" you to act. Extrinsic motivators play directly into our fear of rejection and desire to belong—the part of our cavewoman brain that we discussed earlier—to push us to certain actions so we can avoid the pain of punishment or rejection.

Unsurprisingly, most people (myself included) chase extrinsic expressions of success first. They try to build a business or land a job that makes them seem successful according to the standards society sets. They measure their success via external validation, such as number of followers, level of fame, accumulation of material objects or money.

And, if they don't measure up to the external validators set for them, they feel like they are completely failing at life.

Now—I'm all for extrinsic expression of our life purpose, which is intrinsically motivating in itself. If your life is built around, focused on, and rewarded for the intrinsic life purpose you are expressing externally, then more power to you, sister. But usually it doesn't happen like that overnight. First, we need to find other ways to express our life purpose to build our trust muscle, gain confidence, and become more of our authentic selves.

If we wrap our self-worth up into how much money we make, how many people like and respect us, and how much society-approved success we've gathered—then we will inevitably feel unhappy and unfulfilled.

Instead, we need to focus our efforts first (and, in my opinion, entirely) on our intrinsic expression. We need to identify the ways we can start living our purpose now, ways that aren't tied to any external expectations. Think of it as a quicker, cheaper (most of the time free), and more efficient way to hack the life you've always dreamed of living. Which, when boiled down, is a life of living your purpose.

Benefits of Intrinsic Expressions

So, what does intrinsic expression of purpose look like? Allow me to introduce you to my client Sara.

Sara was also born of immigrant parents who taught her all the values most immigrants teach their kids: Pick a stable career and don't be frivolous with your time or money. She was discouraged from doing most of the things she loved to do until she became an adult and, as many of us do, she started to ask herself deeper questions about the purpose of her life.

In doing so she honored her desire to learn and teach yoga. Sara had a stable career at a tech company, so she wasn't looking to make a major career change. She just wanted to feel happier and more fulfilled in her life, so she started sharing her gift for teaching yoga on social media.

She offered yoga classes via live stream to put her yoga certification to work. She also shares deep insights about personal growth on her posts, as well as raises money for charities. So she is sharing her gifts, her wisdom and making her unique contribution all through doing something she loves.

Her account hasn't blown up (yet), and she's not impacting millions (yet), but the party has started. I asked her what she has gotten out of sharing her gifts (as opposed to talking herself out of expressing them) and she said:

> I am more courageous. I am more authentic with myself. I am more at peace with myself. I am more confident. I am more whole. I believe in myself. I have more energy. I am expanding. I accept myself more. I am contributing to causes I care about. I am more inspired. I am more in alignment.

If this doesn't make a case for honoring your desires and expressing your intrinsic desires regardless of extrinsic rewards, then I don't know what will. By simply sharing her true self and her gifts, she's been rewarded with major benefits.

So you don't get to skip this step. Following your intrinsic desires is the bridge to that extrinsic lifestyle you desire, and crossing that bridge will leave you feeling fulfilled rather than empty. You have to go through this stage and spend time learning how to honor your inner desires, take risks, and trust yourself. Your inner critic will be uncomfortable—but she's just repeating someone else's message anyway.

The only way we can ever create the life we truly desire is by taking full responsibility for it.

Taking Responsibility

When you did your Life Purpose Statement, did you surprise yourself with anything you said you wanted? You never know what your soul is going to say when you take a moment to actually listen. She's a wild stallion, so I can see why we have been scared of her. But honoring her is a truly exciting adventure, and it makes life more worth living.

Okay, on to sexual harassment. Just kidding, but I do want to address something that needs to happen as you embark on living the badass revolutionary life that you deserve. If you are on this path, you must go from being stuck in a mindset of victimhood to one of responsibility. I did, and though it wasn't fun by any means, it was a necessary transformation, one we gotta go through in order to live our purpose.

Three months into my first job out of college I was sexually harassed. This work environment celebrated the girls with big racks and small voices who did what they were told. My voice was huge, and my rack was small, so once again I didn't fit in.

A male coworker who didn't seem to like my sassy personality would jokingly make comments about how I needed to tone it down. I would always snap right back at him. It was ongoing contentious banter.

One day I was sitting at my desk when he walked into my office, closed the door behind him, hovered over me, and said, "If you don't lose your attitude, I am going to bend you over this desk and spank you."

I was jolted by this display of intimidation, but I played the tough girl and told him to get out. I ended up telling my superiors. The CEO in no uncertain terms said, "But he was joking right? You can still work with him, right?"

And, holding back tears, I said yes.

Staying at that job each day after that incident stripped away layer after layer of my dignity. I felt like by staying I was complicit in my own oppression. Remember those unconscious messages? Well, what I was saying to myself was, "It's okay to disrespect me. I can't and won't do anything about it." I was afraid I wouldn't be able to get another job and that quitting early would look bad on my résumé.

So I stayed.

Letting Go of Victim Vibes

I didn't see it then, but now I can clearly see that I was holding on to my role as victim. I was willingly staying in a lukewarm life that I had a big hand in creating by simply not trying to do anything different.

So many of us get stuck there. We feel helpless and victimized by the circumstances in our lives. We blame our parents, our circumstances, our boss, the government, our upbringing, and the era we were born in for why we aren't happy, fulfilled, rich, etcetera.

If you ever want to live an empowered life, you gotta let that shit go.

Once our brains are fully developed, it's our job—and our job alone—to grow out of the reactive and passive role of playing the victim and learn to take responsibility for the direction of our life through the choices we make, the actions we take, and the results we create.

Because taking responsibility for the circumstances you create in your life is the only way you can change it. Taking responsibility is a prerequisite to fulfillment.

I eventually quit that job and moved on to something else, but only after I had attended that cheesy personal development seminar and was introduced to coaching. It was during a three-month program where I had a coach and a community of people who supported me that I finally had the courage to leave that toxic work environment.

I was learning to stand up for what I deserved, which wasn't easy, and I couldn't do it alone. This is why it's imperative for anyone who wants to make lasting change in their life to have a coach and a community, but we will talk more about that in Chapter 9.

This created a huge shift in my life. I finally took responsibility for the fact that it was *my job* to make sure I was treated well in my life. If that CEO wouldn't do it, that was on him. But if I stayed and played by his rules, that was on me. It was not easy; it was scary, and my journey wasn't smooth. But my life was mine, dammit, and I wasn't going to allow myself to be disrespected anymore. And that was everything.

In that moment, what I unconsciously said to my soul was, "I will stand up for you. You matter. I've got your back." It was healing for me, and it was my own internal revolution. After all the programming I had as a child that told me my feelings didn't matter—for the first time, I put a stake in the ground as a grown-ass woman and I said they did. I was no longer a victim, so fulfillment and freedom were mine for the taking.

If you continually view yourself as a victim, you will never be empowered to make change. Whether you're stuck in a dead-end job, a toxic relationship, or a sketchy neighborhood, it's on you to get yourself out. Choosing to stay there makes you complicit in whatever kind of shitstorm you're living.

This radical act of responsibility means facing some harsh truths. It's not easy to look at yourself in the mirror and realize that you are a large part of the reason for all the circumstances that are making you unhappy.

It's not your fault that you are there, but it's your responsibility to get the fuck out. No one will save you. I hate saying that, because it feels mean and like a huge downer.

But taking responsibility for your life is the key to being empowered to live the life you've always wanted.

Gloria Steinem said it best: "The truth will set you free—but first it will piss you off."

Resentment as Suicide

Let's revisit the second massive mistake I was making in my twenties—abandoning who I was in order to survive.

I was reacting to pain in a very human way, protecting myself from it by avoiding the circumstances, situations, decisions, and people who made me uncomfortable. It's natural that we try to shield ourselves from discomfort. But what I learned along the way is that when you block your heart from pain, you also block it from joy.

Let me say that again.

You cannot protect yourself from pain without pushing away joy. They are two sides of the same coin. They come hand in hand. If you choose to block your heart from pain, then expect to live a very apathetic, detached, but painless life. You may feel no pain, but you will also feel somewhat dead inside.

No wonder people who suppressed their feelings were 30 percent more likely to experience premature death and 70 percent more likely to be diagnosed with cancer (pretty sure men need to read this book too, lol).[50]

Although it seemed wise in my very human head to protect myself from pain, what I was doing was actually very self-destructive. Not to mention that it was painful in its own way. Have you ever felt like you were losing yourself?

I was losing myself personally and professionally, and I'll tell you how. Professionally, as I mentioned earlier, I was opting to be a "bitch," to be perceived as strong and tough to gain respect in the corporate environment. Although this felt like the "smart" thing to do, it also subconsciously hurt my heart. I was in a constant state of self-protection, and that felt stressful, not to mention draining.

I didn't feel like I could actually be myself and succeed in that environment. So, if you feel like that anywhere in your life, do yourself a favor and change the environment instead of changing yourself—your heart and soul will thank you, and I'll thank you, too.

Personally, I have always been a woman of integrity. I am fiercely loyal, honest, and trustworthy. I love people and do right by them because I am a very good person. At the same juncture in my life I was struggling personally. After a bad breakup, I found out he had been lying to me about some things, so to get back at him I started to date one of his friends. They weren't best friends; they were acquaintances, but that doesn't make it any better.

I was doing it to hurt him, and I succeeded. At the time, I felt he deserved it. But what did I do to myself in the process?

I compromised who I was. I was being vindictive. I was vengeful, and I was becoming a shittier version of myself. I was resentful of how he did me wrong and decided he had it coming.

There's a quote from Nelson Mandela, "Resentment is like drinking poison and waiting for the other person to die."

At first I thought this was some superdeep, wise, and philosophical idea that was just there to help us all be less of assholes to one another. But after further thought, I realized it's actually a fact.

Research studies have linked resentment to cancer.[51] Participants in these studies reported extremely low anger scores, which usually means a person is suppressing their anger and harboring resentment instead. A lot of evidence connects a mild but chronic feeling of resentment to cancer, and specifically to breast cancer.

Cancer is also linked to stress in the body. Is it so shocking that when your heart is hurting but you won't express it, you get cancer near your heart?

Let's all be ragey-ass bitches together and tear some shit up. JK (but not really). Anger is an emotion (just like any other emotion) that gives us clarity on how something affects us. Emotions are not good or bad; they are just indicators. The more we can notice these indicators (instead of suppressing them), the more we can stay in tune with our inner guidance system. The voice in your head that tells you it's not okay to feel angry is also the voice of the patriarchy. You can ignore it and keep moving forward as a fully expressed human being. Okay, back to the story.

This was a low point for me when I was struggling personally and professionally. I wasn't happy with my career choices, didn't feel like I could be who I truly was, and I found myself becoming more of an asshole because I thought that's what I needed to do to survive.

I was abandoning myself. I was compromising my character. I wasn't being a leader of self or deciding proactively who I wanted to be in the world. I was reacting to pain and creating chaos as a result. This is an expression of that same patriarchal energy that I want us all to heal from.

Instead of having the courage to be who I am or to do what's right regardless of the pain, I was becoming smaller and contorting into someone else as a response to pain. It is a very typical response.

But what should you do instead?

Be the Truth

You can choose to be a leader of self. You can decide that you are strong enough to withstand pain and choose to remain true to your essence. You can be more committed to who you truly are than to protecting yourself from pain.

And let's be honest, pain is inevitable. Even if you do everything you can to live a safe and secure life, shit happens. So the idea that you can avoid pain is a lie.

If pain is inevitable, you might as well go through this life as the pure unaltered version of yourself. Someone who proactively chooses her behaviors and actions according to who she truly is. Honor your essence rather than shrinking back into the scared little girl that you aren't anymore.

Be the bad bitch that you know you are.

One of my favorite Maya Angelou quotes (and there are many) is:

> "Do the best you can until you know better. Then when you know better, do better."

While it's our responsibility to take control of our lives and embrace our authentic selves, there's no point in harping on what we should have done. Up until now you've been operating with only so much information. You've been told by your parents and society to live a certain way. And most importantly, you've been told no. Over and over again.

- No to what you desire.
- No to your creativity.
- No to your emotions.
- No to who you are.

It's no wonder you haven't chased after your dreams and may have settled for less than you deserve. So many of us do.

But just as it's up to you to take responsibility for yourself, it's also up to you to finally be the one who says yes. A resounding YES. You must radically accept all that you truly are and all that you want to experience.

Because when you mimic your parents and continuously tell yourself no, you're peeling a part of your true self away. You're molding yourself into an expectation instead of being the truth. You're engaging in what, ultimately, is the slow and painful death of your soul.

If you do the other thing—say yes to yourself and be the truth of who you are—it's very life-giving. You're empowered, confident, and ready to go after what it is you want.

With the tools and guides in this book, you'll know better. And then it's up to you to promise yourself to do better.

— Life Work —

Let's get clear on your truth so that you can go about the business of being it. Grab a journal and a pen and let's get to work.

1. Where in your life are you protecting yourself from pain?
2. How is this blocking you from receiving love?
3. How is this self-protection compromising your ability to express your true essence?
4. What is something in your life currently that makes you feel hurt or angry?
5. How does it hurt you to suppress those feelings?
6. How would you do things differently if you weren't afraid of any repercussions?

Message me what you plan to do differently as a result of reading this chapter and share your Life Purpose Statement with me as well.

My email is shereen@shereenthor.com. I look forward to hearing how you are revolutionizing your life. Xo.

5
DITCH
People Pleasing

> *Care about what other people think and you will always be their prisoner.*
> —Lao Tzu

*I*f you want to awaken your rebel and make a difference in this world, you must first heal from codependent tendencies. Nobody likes labels, and you may be slightly annoyed that I'm assuming you're codependent. But I have my reasons.

First, you are a woman. Women are nurturers by nature. We're the gender that loves to give and give and then give a little more, a symptom of codependence. And as you learned in earlier chapters (and likely in your own life), this genetic generosity has been taken advantage of in more ways than one.

I've worked with thousands of clients, and the majority of them have experienced codependency even if they didn't realize that's what it was at the time. Although being a woman is not necessarily a determining factor of this emotional and behavioral condition, it does make codependency more likely.

The second reason I'm assuming you need to heal from codependency is that you picked up this book, which was written by a recovering codependent (hi). Some intuitive part of you knows the teachings included here will support you in an impactful way. (Your soul knows what you need and unconsciously guides you; you should thank her—she's so bad.)

I have coached all different types of women, and though this may seem like a grandiose claim, I'm going to make it anyway:

Whether you're a walking doormat, a boss chick, or a woman hanging out somewhere in between, codependency is likely sucking the life out of you on some level.

At one end of the spectrum are the super obvious people pleasers, who struggle to assert themselves. They overthink every syllable that comes out of their mouth. They're desperate to go with the flow and keep the boat unrocked. And when they do finally stand up for themselves—even if it's as tiny a stance as saying no to eating at a restaurant they hate—they feel horrible.

At the other end of the spectrum are these hella powerhouse boss chicks who seem like the farthest thing from codependent. They're kicking ass, taking names, and have zero issues making dinner plans. But when you do some digging into their psyche and learn what drives them (and what holds them back), you'll find there's an inner people pleaser who's burning the candle at both ends to prove she's worthy. This type of codependency is more insidious and harder to detect, but trust me, it's the same issue rearing its ugly head.

Codependency shows up differently in everyone. Sometimes it's more apparent, like refusing to leave a verbally abusive boyfriend. And sometimes it's more subtle, like being the last one to leave work because you are a workaholic. These behaviors look very different, but they're actually quite similar underneath. They're just on opposite sides of the same codependent coin.

So, whether you are like, "I am a people pleaser—help me!" Or you're thinking, "I am not a people pleaser at all—I run the show," you need this chapter.

Still not convinced you're codependent? See how many of these characteristics of codependent people you can relate to:[52]

- An exaggerated sense of responsibility for the actions of others
- A tendency to confuse love and pity and the tendency to "love" people they can pity and rescue
- A tendency to do more than their share, all of the time (Remember that statistic on how a woman who's the breadwinner will still do 90 percent of the housework? Ahem.)
- A tendency to become hurt when people don't recognize their efforts
- An unhealthy dependence on relationships and a willingness to do anything to hold on to a relationship or avoid the feeling of abandonment
- An extreme need for approval and recognition
- A sense of guilt when asserting themselves
- A compelling need to control others
- Lack of trust in self and/or others
- Fear of being abandoned or alone
- Difficulty identifying feelings
- Rigidity/difficulty adjusting to change
- Problems with intimacy/boundaries
- Chronic anger
- Lying/dishonesty
- Poor communications
- Difficulty making decisions

All of these are typical signs of codependency, which Mental Health America refers to as "an emotional and behavioral condition that affects an individual's ability to have a healthy, mutually satisfying relationship."[53] It may seem dramatic or unsettling to refer to your fear of abandonment or your lack of trust in yourself as a mental health condition, but don't worry. These common behaviors are learned, which means they can be unlearned.

Codependency is also referred to as "relationship addiction" because people who are codependent often can maintain only one-sided relationships. And those tend to be toxic and/or emotionally, physically, or mentally abusive relationships at that.

Although our society educates us on algebra and grammar, it gives us zero education on how to have healthy relationships. Be it with your mother, your partner, your best friend, or your Hinge date, understanding how to navigate personal connections with other humans is one of the major lessons we must all learn for our personal and professional success.

In addition to how awful living with codependency *feels* emotionally, research shows that it can also severely impact our physical health. Scientists studied 505 family members who displayed a high level of codependency with their drug-user family members (codependents and addicts are homies).[54] They found that a high level of codependency "imposed a significant burden on the physical and emotional well-being of those affected, resulting in poor health, reactivity, self-neglect and additional responsibilities."

Another study revealed a link between codependency and depression: If a person reports themselves to be highly codependent, they're also likely to experience elevated levels of depression.[55]

And no studies or scientists need to tell you that codependent relationships are often toxic and can put the codependent in violent and potentially dangerous situations.

So, yes, healing from codependency and creating a new way of being are absolutely imperative to finding your calling in life and keeping your body in good health so that you can live long and prosper. Consider healing from codependency to be the prerequisite to living your purpose and finding your happy.

If you're too concerned with other people's opinions of you, then it's nearly impossible to hear your own soul speak. Not to mention all the relational shenanigans you are wasting your life force on. And, yes, I mean life *force*. You are a force to be reckoned with (why do you think we've been oppressed for centuries?). You're scary powerful, and it's revolutionary to allow that power to shine. Healing from codependency is a massive step in the direction of returning to your essence.

You must let go of the toxic patterns you keep finding yourself in so you can say yes to your purpose. You need to let go of what other people think of you in order to say yes to your purpose. And finally, you need to give your energy to activities and behaviors that are life-giving so that you can avoid the depression and burnout codependents inevitably experience. There is basically no way you can live a happy, fulfilled, healthy life if you are codependent.

So, let's ditch that shit.

The Broken Hero

When you are codependent, you're always living for other people. You're fulfilling their desires or agendas. You're running their errands. You're attending their social events. You're doing whatever you can to make their lives easier, and often this comes at the expense of your own.

You're so busy tuning in to what they need that you're actively ignoring what *you* need.

People who are codependent want to make everyone else happy. They're the self-proclaimed heroes of the world who exist solely to save all the broken birds in life. It's no surprise that they do this because their self-worth is wrapped up in how much they can help others.

But when your self-worth depends on other people needing and loving you, it crumbles when they don't love or need you anymore. And when that happens, a codependent becomes deeply unhappy, depressed, and anxious.

Who am I if they don't need me anymore?
Who am I if I can't be there for them anymore?
Who am I?

You see this a lot with overly attached mothers. At a glance it looks like love, but after further inspection you see that the mother needs to be needed so much that they are enabling, preventing their child from becoming independent. It's less of a service to their offspring and more of an addiction being fulfilled.

Codependent people also secretly feel chronically undervalued. In the most honest moments with clients who have codependent tendencies here are some examples of what they share:

I'm always showing up for everyone else, and no one ever shows up for me.
Everybody secretly hates me and thinks I'm a bad person.
If I tell this person how I really feel, they'll never talk to me again.
It doesn't matter if I don't get what I want as long as they are happy because I'm afraid they'll leave me otherwise.
Nobody looks out for me as much as I look out for them.
I'm always left behind.
I'm alone.

The problem with codependency is that you are hoping your gas tank will get filled by emptying it. It's a backward recipe. The emptier it feels, the more you run on fumes, trying harder to please in an effort to fill your tank. It only empties more.

An obsession with making sure everyone else is happy—and thus never prioritizing your own happiness—is a recipe for depression. And a completely unsustainable way to live. Whether you address this issue now or ten years from now, at some point it's going to rear its ugly, clingy head and demand your attention.

If you're identifying a lot with this, don't worry. You're not alone. A lot of people, including myself at one point, have lived this way.

I did it when I chose a career to appease my mother instead of following my heart.

I did it when I went broke as a newbie entrepreneur overpaying business coaches who underdelivered because I didn't trust myself.

I did it as a new mom when I prioritized my husband's freedom and happiness over my own.

We all do it in some form or another—so thanks for the algebra lesson, but I'm pretty sure I needed Healthy Relationships 101 instead. Recognizing and healing these patterns are some of the most important things a woman can do to get her power back and get back on the yellow brick road to happiness, success, fulfillment, and self-actualization.

At my core I am deeply obsessed with empowering women to empower themselves. I don't want to save them. I want them to learn to save themselves. That's what this entire book is about. But you will never be able to save yourself if your self-worth comes from something outside of you.

So let's begin the work of healing.

Upgrade Your Operating System

Most of my clients come to me for reasons other than healing their codependency issues. In fact, many aren't aware they are codependent at all. But as we work toward achieving their dream career, their ideal relationship, or their optimal self-care routine, it always comes up. No matter what their self-proclaimed problems are, no matter where they feel stuck in their life, healing from codependency is usually the answer.

One of my clients, we'll call her Sheila, has been married to a man she loves for five years—and her parents STILL don't know. They never approved of this man, and because of their disapproval, she never mentioned her nuptials. They think he's just her boyfriend.

Because she doesn't want to disappoint her parents, Sheila has taken it upon herself to live out dual lives, the one she wants, and the one her parents are willing to accept. She feels like she has to be who they want her to be in order to be accepted by her family, and it's no surprise that she struggles to juggle all those balls, which inevitably drains her energetically.

Another example is Melissa, who dates disrespectful men for much longer than she wants to because she feels too guilty to tell them she's not interested. We are talking years and years of her life with men she is not that into because the idea of saying no or establishing a boundary is more frightening than enduring bad treatment.

We may be looking at these two as extreme examples, but women do these kinds of things to themselves all the time in big and often small ways. It's innate. We are taught to sit pretty, smile nice, and not cause a fuss. We're rewarded when we put the needs, feelings, and desires of others before our own. So, we do what we are told and suffer in silence.

If left unchecked, these codependent tendencies will ruin your life. When you feel the need to give everybody everything and you can't say no or ask for what you want, you're no longer a human. You're just the world's most overworked, underpaid personal assistant.

A queen living like a servant.

The lack of confidence and self-worth results from the belief we picked up at a young age, typically in our family of origin, that our wants and needs should be put on the backburner in favor of what other people need.

But here's the thing: You're grown. That mode of operating worked in your formative years because that's the skill set you needed to survive in that environment. That survival tactic is currently harming you in your adult life, so it's time for things to change. The paradigms you adopted back then to survive no longer work when it's time to thrive.

It's time to upgrade your operating system.

When my clients reveal their struggles and I share about codependency, I have to (1) explain what codependency means and (2) teach them how to prioritize their needs. That act of radical self-honoring can look like ordering a pizza when your husband is demanding Chinese. It can look like starting that side hustle you've been daydreaming about. It can look like canceling plans with that friend who never fails to make you feel like shit.

It's about honoring your true desires on a daily basis. Saying yes to yourself more often than you say no.

Telling the people who have grown reliant on your fabulous people-pleasing skills that from now on you will be focusing on pleasing yourself and that you trust they are capable of taking care of themselves.

It's harder than it sounds, especially because you are saying no to something that used to be perceived as the thing that made you valuable. But slowly, one revolutionary act at a time, you will transform from a burnt-out people pleaser to a self-expressed queen who values herself regardless of what others may think of her.

It's also worth noting that there's a difference between helping someone and being drained by someone. Some people don't want to be saved. So, you as the codependent are often trying to save a drowning person who would much rather sink. People often repeat and re-create past traumas, living them out over and over again, and sometimes have no intention of moving forward. That's their choice. By engaging with these types, you become a supply for them to feed off of while they literally suck the life out of you.

Many codependents do this as well: They get stuck in a downward spiral of constantly saving the unsavable—but not you. You picked up this book, so I know you are onto some bigger shit. When you stop emptying yourself out on other people's agendas, you will absolutely revolutionize your life. And the life will give you what you need to heal through it. Here's a juicy little story about how life handed me a situation that required me to heal from codependency.

The Universe Has Your Back

A trademark behavior of a codependent person is always being there for other people. Being the one everyone can lean on. The *strong one*.

I learned early on that I needed to not be a burden because my single immigrant mother was tired and tapped. That grew to form much of my identity. For some reason, I became the unofficial therapist among family and friends. I put on a strong face and spoke at my dad's funeral at the age of seventeen. I saved my sister (or at least I tried to) every time she was dating a dick. I signed myself up for the task of solving problems for a countless number of friends and boyfriends.

I built my identity on being the counselor, the helper, the savior, and a lot of my self-worth was wrapped up in how much I could help others and never ask for anything in return. I was a giver. Easy to be around, always full of laughs and great advice. I was who everyone needed me to be.

This worked for me as a young person. It made me very well liked and popular. However, as I have said before, what we learn to do in our youth to survive is not what we need to do as adults to thrive.

After meeting the love of my life in my late twenties, I quickly made the transition from the single-cool-chick-employee to wife-mom-entrepreneur all in the course of one year.

This seemed exciting because many of my dreams were coming true. But in my old paradigm, success and self-sufficiency went hand in hand. I was convinced that I had to be the strong one for everyone else (as I had in the past) and that I should never be a burden if I wanted to be loved.

Vulnerability was a muscle I never flexed. Asking for help felt like a death sentence. I had certainly learned to be more authentic and to express who I was in my years of awakening my rebel. But I had NOT learned how to shed codependent patterns. I still wanted everyone to think that I was superwoman.

Remember that statistic about how people who suppress their feelings are 30 percent more likely to experience premature death and 70 percent more likely to be diagnosed with cancer?

I was on the road to experiencing one (or both) of those disastrous effects—until I got knocked up. During my first pregnancy, I was put on doctor-ordered bed rest. I hated it, rebelled against it, and created a lot of suffering as a result of my inability to relax. Unsurprisingly, once my daughter was born, I struggled with postpartum depression, certainly a result of hormones and chemicals but also because I kept trying to do it all alone, which was my old operating system.

I wanted my husband to still be able to play football on Saturdays—God forbid his life be inconvenienced by us starting a family. I thought I could stay up all night with my colicky baby, do coach calls, build a business, and just keep it moving like nothing had happened. Looking back, this makes me want to punch myself directly in the face.

I acted like I didn't need anything, so no one gave me anything. And let me tell you, I fucking suffered. This was the bleakest and most depressing time of my entire life. I struggled tremendously and became suicidal four weeks after giving birth.

Now I have a very intense visceral memory of what life feels like when I deprioritize my needs in favor of everyone else's. This is a reference point that reminds me never to go back to my codependent tendencies. There I was, suddenly responsible for the life of another human, I needed help more than ever, but I was too stubborn to ask.

This was the most in-your-face way that life could teach me to quit it with my BS superhero vibes and admit that I am human. I have needs, and they deserve to be met—or bad things will happen not only to me but to my baby as well.

Both of my pregnancies were at-risk pregnancies for preterm labor, so I was put on bed rest for five to six months each time. This was a doctor's order to slow down, be vulnerable, and learn to receive support in order to have a healthy baby.

If you need a codependent to heal, don't make it about them. Make it about the baby or about another person and see how quickly they go from selfless to "selfish." Making it about the baby's well-being gave me, a codependent, the perfect justification so that I didn't have to feel guilty for being "needy." And as I read this now, I realize how sad it is that I thought I needed a justification at all. Another reason I wrote this book, I don't want you to need to justify your needs. I just want you to feel free to get them met.

The universe really did give me exactly what I needed to upgrade my operating system. Which makes that whole cliché "The Universe has got your back" feel less like a cliché and more like a universal truth. Whether you believe in God or the Universe or Buddha, I hope you are picking up what I'm putting down.

I slowly rehabilitated myself and my life, one choice at a time. I learned to say yes to myself more than I said no. I learned eventually how to let others deal with disappointment rather than taking on too much responsibility for their feelings and hurting myself in the process.

As a wife, mother, and entrepreneur, my new life needed a new version of me to thrive. So I upgraded my operating system. And now it's time for you to upgrade yours.

You're Worth It

If the idea of standing up for yourself makes you want to crawl into a dark hole and live there, I get it. Healing from codependency is terrifying when all you've ever wanted to do is make other people happy and not rock the boat.

But living your truth is your responsibility as a human on this planet. When you live for others at your own expense, you're robbing the world of your authenticity, your gifts, your contributions. You are giving people a false version of yourself so that in actuality they don't even know who you truly are. No wonder you feel so alone and misunderstood.

Here's the thing, we recovering people pleasers often think we are being "nice" by giving people whatever they want at our own expense. But these kinds of relationships are not nice, they are abusive and one-sided. So stop fooling yourself into thinking that you're doing the world a favor by dishonoring yourself. Do I need to remind you of the statistics or the number one regret of the dying? That shit ain't nice.

You need to step into the truth of who you are. Awaken to your life's purpose and self-actualize. Feel the power of being yourself versus being what everyone else wants you to be. And that, my darling, is a revolutionary act.

It's Okay to Be Bad

If you could put my entire philosophy on healing from codependency in a nutshell, it would be this:

It's okay to be bad.

It's okay to disappoint other people. It's okay to make other people mad. It's okay if your mom disapproves of your career choice and your dad hates your haircut. It's okay.

The first time I decided to actively rebel against my mother's expectations by becoming a comedian, I knew I had to be okay with her disapproval. I was certain she would hate this choice, so I was sort of forced to accept the consequences ahead of time. It turns out, accepting that I was going to be seen as "bad" was the all-in-one magic medicine I needed to heal from codependency as a whole.

Of course, I didn't recognize that right away. I've had many a doormat moment when I allowed someone to convince me my boundaries made me a bad or mean person. And then I'd run back to that person again and again in increasingly desperate attempts to make them believe I was indeed a good person (SMH, FML).

So, please, my dear ex–people pleaser, know that you don't always have to be a "good" person. You don't always have to be the wonderful human being who sacrifices everything for everyone at a moment's notice. You, just like everyone else in the world, can have needs, desires, impulses, and boundaries.

This is why my entire brand was built on the idea of awakening your rebel. Through giving myself permission to be perceived as "bad," I was giving myself freedom. This idea of being the good girl, or being obedient, must be dissected a bit because it can unknowingly lead to a terrible cycle of abuse.

The Cycle of Abuse

Many codependents can't stand being viewed as bad or mean (I was one of them). I would go back to my abusers to get the validation I was desperately seeking. To prove to them that I was in fact a good person.

All you needed to do to get me to be your forever-love type of doormat was make me out to be a villain. Damn, that shit worked like a charm. I would crawl back for more and more and more and more, relentlessly trying to prove that I was good, not bad. And I would take more abuse in the process. It was a vicious cycle.

I mostly experienced this with my sister growing up. God bless her heart, I know she means well, but holy shit did we engage in this cycle. One summer when I was home from college, I stored my furniture from my apartment in my mom's garage. My sister had a friend who needed a couch, so without asking me, she let her friend take mine.

When I got home and saw that my couch was gone, I asked her where it was. She said, "My friend needed a couch, so I gave it to her." I was *so* pissed. That was my fucking couch, and she just gave it away?! Who in the fuck gives away someone else's furniture?! What in the fuck am I going to sit on when I move back to school?! I felt so violated.

It was a feeling I was familiar with in our relationship. She was older than me and had likely become accustomed to having free rein over whatever I perceived as "mine." When I told her how inappropriate that was and that she should get the couch back for me, she didn't like it.

Instead of taking responsibility for how she was wrong and apologizing (which would have been awesome), she made me out to be a bad person for "not understanding who she truly is."

She was trying to make the claim that if I had a problem with her actions, then I must not truly know her heart. She shut me out because I was being so "mean" to her. Slammed a door in my face. Textbook gaslighting.

So then, I was feeling violated, and on top of that I was being punished for standing up for myself. This was fucked up on her part, and total abuse. But it was me who went back for more.

I tried to prove to her that I wasn't a mean person. I tried to explain to her that I knew her heart, but that I still didn't want to be treated this way. She shut me out again and again. She screamed at me (I screamed back, of course). She did whatever she needed to do to get me to shut the fuck up. And it worked. It worked every fucking time. Just like it had worked for years.

All she had to do was make me out to be the bad guy (even if I wasn't) and I would fold. My inner people pleaser just couldn't stomach being viewed as "mean." By folding, I was allowing myself to be abused. Just like I was allowing myself to be disrespected at my first job. Just like I allowed myself to become depressed as a young mother.

I learned to fold early on in my life, and I developed a terribly codependent tendency of needing approval more than I needed justice.

But here's the thing: It was my job to stand up for myself.

Hear me now: It is your job to stand up for yourself.

Regardless of what people think of you. It's okay if they disapprove. Freedom is only yours if you are willing to stomach disapproval. This was a vicious cycle of abuse, and it was caused—not by the abuser—but by my low self-esteem.

If I cared more about what I thought of myself than what she thought of me, I never would have been abused in the first place. And the same goes for you.

You will never gain anyone's respect unless you respect yourself. You will never gain validation by caring about what others think of you. You will only gain the approval of others once you truly approve of yourself.

If you want to heal from codependency, you have to be okay with people thinking ill of you in the moment because you're not fulfilling their agenda. And you have to figure out what you think of yourself so that your inner voice is louder than the outer voices; it's just the way it works. And trust me, once you begin to actively heal your codependency, a lot of people won't like you for it.

Relationships in your life will reshuffle and change, and when they do, I need you to remember that it's totally okay. Someone who no longer likes you for becoming healthy is not a healthy person.

It also proves that you're evolving, and your relationships must evolve, too. If a friend only likes the people-pleaser version of you, aren't they kind of a shitty friend? If someone is in your life for what you can do for them or how you can make them feel, then they've got to GO. They are just a version of your old way of relating with others, and they don't belong in your life anymore.

This will feel uncomfortable (especially because approval is so important to us reforming codependents), but it is a necessary step in your growth toward being the version of you that can thrive rather than simply survive.

I can promise you that those moments of discomfort are more than worth the lifetime of happiness that self-advocacy can bring. The path of healing looks different for everyone, but one thing that is inevitable is that you must learn to set better boundaries. But before we get into boundaries, I want to make sure you avoid the cycle of abuse by avoiding the blame game.

The Villain and the Victim

It would be easy to hear that story and view my sister as the villain and me as the victim. But I want to remind you that placing blame is the same expression of oppression we are trying to transcend. To view her as the villain would be to perpetuate the system that created these issues in the first place.

There is a cliché saying, "Hurt people hurt people." She, just like all of us, is not a villain but a person who had experienced her own set of pain and trauma and hadn't yet healed through it. She has healed tremendously throughout the years, and we have a much healthier relationship now. We have all at one point or another been the abuser and the abusee. Remember my story about how I dated my boyfriend's friend? I was hurt, and I was attempting to hurt him in return.

I hadn't yet awoken from my toxic slumber. I was still a product of the sick society I was born into, so I was perpetuating the system. Just as we all have perpetuated it at one point or another. It is not our fault, but it *is* our responsibility to awaken out of this toxic sleep and transcend these unhealthy patterns to create a better world.

If we look past my sister to try to place blame, we will see my mother and try to blame her. But when you hear her story, you remember that she was first abused by my father. Then he's the one! He must be the villain in this story. But when you hear his story, you will see that he was also abused and had his own set of pain and trauma he was dealing with.

In order to break the cycle of abuse, we must first let go of this need to blame. We must understand that we are all fucked up because we have been fucked up by someone or something that has caused us pain or trauma. There are no victims and there are no villains, there are only flawed human beings all trying to survive in this sick society.

You will make no progress in placing blame. Breaking the cycle of abuse requires us to release the need to condemn, and then we can heal from within. We must take responsibility for ourselves and how we engage in this cycle so that we have the power to change it. This is how we can transcend our sick society, let go of toxic paradigms, and unplug from the matrix.

A Caveat

Taking responsibility for what you create and allow in your life is not the same as bypassing your pain. In order to heal, you must first admit someone did you wrong. Then you can feel and process the pain. This means you may feel like a victim for a moment, and I encourage you to give yourself that right. It is the only way to truly heal and forgive in order to move forward.

If you bypass the truth of your experience, you will remain stuck because what you resist persists. If you acknowledge and allow your feelings to come to the surface, then you can process them and let them go. This is painful and hard to do alone, so it can be helpful to have the support of a therapist or coach.

You are responsible for what you create in your life, so although it may not be your fault, it *is* your responsibility to lead yourself toward the light rather than re-creating darkness. Once you have taken responsibility for what you create in your own life, the easiest way to ensure healthier relationships moving forward is through having healthy boundaries. So let's get this party started.

Boundaries Are the New Black

As a recovering codependent, I've had a rollercoaster-esque relationship with setting boundaries. For the majority of my life, I had none. The line where my identity ended and another person's began was blurred beyond recognition. All I wanted to do was help others, and I was more than willing to lose myself in the process.

When I started my journey in personal development, I realized how important healthy boundaries are. Not only do they help us form our identity and gain true agency over our life, but they also lead to better relationships and keep us from falling into old unhealthy patterns from the past.

If you don't have boundaries, you allow yourself to be at the total mercy of other people. Their mood swings, their messes, their melodrama—all of it becomes the compass by which you direct your life (Lord have mercy).

When you *do* set strong boundaries to protect your time, energy, and values, life becomes easier to manage. The people in your life get a clear picture of what you will and will not put up with. They learn to respect that you're not their personal chauffeur or on-call therapist. And the ones who don't quickly fall by the wayside (let 'em go).

While most of us are familiar with the concept of boundaries, it can be hard to see what they look like in reality. So I put together a little pop quiz to see how strong healthy boundaries are in your life. Answer yes or no to the following:

1. I feel compelled to answer every new call, text, or email no matter what I'm doing.
2. I often have to restructure my schedule because someone asked me to do something.
3. Most of the conversations I have with loved ones and friends are one-sided (all about them).
4. I feel guilty if I do anything even remotely selfish (e.g., get a drink from Starbucks *without* calling my husband to see if he wants anything).
5. I'm quick to cancel plans if they don't line up with what someone else wants to do.

If you answered yes to any or all of these statements, then you could use stronger boundaries. But don't sweat it, girlfriend, we got this.

How to Set Boundaries Without Being an Asshole

Many people associate boundaries with separateness. We think that it means cutting ourselves off from other people as if we left our phone at home and we feel naked and detached. But in reality, setting boundaries can bring you *closer* to others, not push you farther away.

When you have strong boundaries, you're showing up as your most authentic self. You're clearly communicating what you need to be happy and fulfilled. You're not hiding behind passive aggression or fake smiles. You're being real. And in doing so you're sharing who you truly are and inviting others to do the same.

This doesn't mean you can never soften your boundaries. In certain relationships and situations you'll feel safe enough to reveal a part of yourself that not everyone has access to.

Boundaries are meant to be fluid and evolving. They can change. The point isn't to set them and never speak of it again. Rather, setting boundaries protects you from relationships and situations that leave you feeling depleted so that instead you can take impeccable care of your inner queen.

Check this out.

Step 1. Identify your core values.

If you find that at the end of most days you're left feeling totally depleted and exhausted, chances are you're allowing your core values to be violated or bypassed. If you want to maintain consistent energy and contentment in life, you have to protect your top three to five values at all times.

If you don't know what your core values are, check out this list of core values: shereenthor.com/values.

Narrow the list down to your top five, and answer the following questions for each:

How often are you allowing this core value to be violated or ignored? In what ways are you currently allowing this to happen in your life?

Step 2. Set boundaries around those values.

Now that you're aware of what your core values are and how they're being violated in your life, it's time to set some boundaries to protect them so you can show up as your highest self. Figure out where to draw the line.

Remember: These boundaries can ebb and flow throughout your life and relationships. Use them as a starting point and make sure to check in regularly on how having a boundary has made you feel.

Setting a boundary is simply putting a limit on what's violating your values. For example, say one of your core values is freedom (I suspect this will be the case for the many rebels who read this). Your boss consistently violates that freedom by texting you after work hours.

Setting a boundary to protect your freedom looks like this: I will not answer any emails, texts, or calls from my boss when I am off the clock.

Here's another example. Say, one of your core values is friendship, and your husband ignores how much you value your friends by always making you feel guilty when you go visit them. To protect that value, you can create a boundary by deciding that once a week, you'll get together with at least one friend.

You can set as many boundaries as you like for each of your values—and you're not limited to just five! Starting with a smaller number can be easier, but it's always a good idea to revisit your values periodically and see which boundaries can be put in place to protect your life force—because that's what this is all about.

Step 3. Communicate your boundaries.
Now comes the fun part! And by *fun* I mean uncomfortable and maybe a little scary. But communicating your boundaries is a crucial step. Without doing this, your boundaries are basically nonexistent.

Why? Boundaries that are unenforced are no boundaries at all. Plain and simple.

Once you have your boundaries set and written out, it's time to have a few conversations—and also set up some reminders to make sure each boundary is super clear because humans are humans, and more likely than not, they'll forget.

Using the examples above, you need to tell your boss that you will answer any messages he/she/they send you after hours once you're back in the office. You can set up a means of communicating about really urgent issues, but personally, I think that unless you're a brain surgeon, nothing is so urgent that it can't wait until nine a.m. Monday morning.

When you have a boundary conversation, stick to using "I" statements. It helps to prevent the blame game and can make boundary setting a little easier. Here's a template to help:

I feel _____ when _____
because _____.
What I need is _____.

Here's a real-life example: I feel hurt and disrespected when you don't stick to our financial agreements because in order for me to feel safe in this marriage I need to be able to trust you. What I need is for us to separate our money a bit more so that I can feel more in control of my financial stability.

Here's another one: I feel hurt when you text me mean things after getting triggered because it feels like I'm being attacked. What I need is for you to wait until you are not triggered anymore to resolve conflict with me. Or I need you to see a therapist weekly so that you can work on your anger.

You get to draw lines in the sand regarding what is and what isn't proper treatment in your opinion. It's up to you to make sure you are treated well, so feel free to truly think about what you want. Oftentimes, this is where therapy or coaching can be supportive because you can get honest about what you really want and get your head on straight before addressing the person you are experiencing the conflict with.

After that conversation is over, it's best to set up a fail-safe: something to remind everyone of your boundary if they try to cross it. Setting up an away message in your email that says "I'm available to answer emails M–F" is a great example, as is putting your phone on Do Not Disturb between five p.m. and nine a.m.

It may take a few attempts at someone trying to break the boundary to solidify its existence, but the longer you stick to your guns, the easier it will be for other people to respect them. Sometimes, though, when it's not as simple as communicating your boundary and then enforcing it, you have go into full-on conflict resolution mode, especially in long-term relationships.

Reforming codependents loathe conflict. We fear rocking the boat for fear of displeasing others—and that's exactly what you need to learn to do. So in this next chapter, I'll teach you how to handle conflict in a way that encourages healing, promotes peace, and creates a level of authenticity in your relationships that you might have only dreamed of.

— Life Work —

Let's take stock of your relationships. Grab a journal and a pen and let's get to work. In these quiet moments with yourself, do yourself a favor and be 100 percent honest. It's the only way to truly change your life.

1. Who has been the biggest abuser in your life?

    a. How have you been complicit in this cycle of abuse?

    b. If you were to awaken the rebel (i.e., be okay with their disapproval), how would you be different with them?

    c. Are you ready to put more stock into what you think of yourself than what others think of you?

    d. Make a list of all the relationships in your life, and designate which ones give you energy versus drain you.

2. Identify your top five values using this tool: shereenthor.com/values

3. Set boundaries around those values as directed earlier in this chapter.

4. Communicate those boundaries to really get the party started.

5. Imagine you were a barbarian in a past life, or some other form of a scary being (have fun here). Allow this version of you to be the enforcer of your boundaries moving forward, and give this alter ego a name. Journal on how that version of you will protect you from here on out.

Remember, nothing changes until you take action on what you learn. So, do the journaling to take stock of the relationships in your life, whether they're personal or professional. And after taking stock, let's get to work. You're worth it.

6

FIGHT
Like a Queen

Nobody can give you freedom. Nobody can give you equality or justice or anything. If you're a (wo)man, you take it.
—Malcolm X

When we're kids, we're told about white picket fences and happily ever afters. As nice as growing up, finding the perfect job, marrying the perfect partner, and living a long, tragedy-free life sounds, it's never close to what we actually get.

We learn pretty quickly that life is full of as many hardships as happy times, and often our go-to method of dealing with that realization is to resist. We ignore it. Sweep it under the rug. Push it away, and pretend that we're fine.

Ignoring conflict in the moment feels like we're doing something right. We're preventing outbursts and arguments by "letting things go."

But acting like everything is okay when inside you know it's not is an act of emotional suicide, and that's not how a queen rolls.

Historically, queens never bowed down to someone else dictating the rules to them.

Queens know their worth and they advocate for their truth. Even if that means going to war. The last thing a queen would ever do is "suck it up" and move along without feeling heard or considered. Oh hell no.

I've been there. I've spent most of my life learning, working, teaching, and making a career out of how to attain happiness. Clearly, I'm obsessed. For the longest time, I believed the road to happiness was freedom. So naturally I focused on making more money as an entrepreneur in order to attain that freedom, love, connection, success, etcetera. I pushed all of the uncomfortable feelings aside because I thought that if my attention landed on negativity, then I would "attract" more negativity. Clearly, I had watched *The Secret* one too many times. So I bypassed any negative feelings in favor of success and progress.

This is more unhealthy mind trash from the racist patriarchy.

My generation and the generations that follow mine have grown a little too scared. We've let ourselves become so comfortable that we actively avoid anything that creates discomfort. That's all fine and dandy if you want to live a boring life where your only communication strategy is ghosting. But if you want to live your truth, be authentic, and feel true freedom, you must be willing to experience discomfort. Even lean into it a little bit.

You've got to learn how to fight like a queen.

Some of the worst moments in my life have been the most illuminating. It wasn't until I was depressed postpartum and suicidal that I could finally open up my eyes and see how I needed to grow.

Although it was hard, I'm so incredibly grateful for those moments. They set the stage for the necessary pivot that moved me into the life of my dreams. They broke me down and remade me into the rebelling, revolutionary queen I am today (super humble brag). They catapulted me into a new way of being.

And now, it's your turn. In this chapter, I'm going to show you exactly what it means to embody the energy of the queen so that you can navigate even the messiest of situations like the royalty that you are. But first, how does our brain perceive conflict?

In Physical Danger

I am certified in conflict mediation and have mediated conflicts in small claims court, in professional settings, in personal settings, and clearly in my own life. While a lot of the examples in this book are personal, there is much to be said for how conflict shows up in work or social situations as well.

The SCARF Model by David Rock is based on neuroscience research. It illustrates that we respond in five domains in social situations, and these five domains activate the same threat and reward responses in our brain that we rely on for physical survival.[56] The five domains are:

1. Status— our relative importance to others
2. Certainty— our relative ability to predict the future
3. Autonomy—our sense of control over events
4. Relatedness—how safe we feel with others
5. Fairness—how fair we perceive the exchanges between people to be

In an interaction with another person, if any of the domains are activated—if, for example, your sense of autonomy is threatened or your sense of fairness is met—understanding the primitive brain response helps us understand why we have such strong emotional reactions when conflict arises. For example, if we were left out of a group activity, we might perceive it as a threat to our status and relatedness. Research shows that this response can stimulate the same region of the brain as physical pain. Our brain perceives it as if we are in physical danger, and so our body releases cortisol, a stress hormone, into our blood, which negatively affects our ability to be solution oriented because we feel threatened.

This signals the fight, flight, or freeze response, and based on how women were socialized, what do you think we typically do?

You Gotta Have the Tits

Codependency, people pleasing, it's all the same. If you've grown up with the mindset that your happiness, preferences, safety, and well-being come last and you don't do your part to change your way of thinking, that soul-crushing pattern of people pleasing is going to show up again and again until you do.

I know firsthand.

In my household, it was my mom's way or the highway. She had a very militant style of parenting that taught me that the only way for me to exist in a peaceful relationship was to step to the side.

This mindset helped me stay out of many conflicts in my childhood, but it nearly led to a divorce in my marriage. The operating system that helped me survive in my childhood was no longer helping in my adulthood. It was time for me to upgrade that operating system so that I could thrive.

My husband, Kenny, is a lovely human. When we started dating our relationship was so much healthier than anything I had experienced before. But even though he was kind and we were super in love, that didn't spare us from our emotional baggage (spoiler alert: it never does).

As an undiagnosed people pleaser codependent, I thought making relationships work meant that I did whatever I could to make the other person happy and comfortable. This is what was true in my childhood, and it turned into an unspoken agreement Kenny and I unconsciously made.

We got along swimmingly for three years until we got married and started having kids. Then that unspoken agreement became outdated as we had our first child and grew as a family. Maya was a challenging, colicky baby from the moment she entered the world. She cried through feedings, showers, and pretty much every other moment she wasn't sleeping. In fact, she didn't sleep that great either, and the sleep deprivation was torturous.

She required so much, and even though it was the hardest time in my life, I truly believe life handed me this little badass baby so that I would expand in my ability to ask for and receive support from my partner so that we could have a healthier partnership. Life handed me the perfect scenario to invite me to grow in the ways I needed most. To grow into a woman who had the tits to advocate for her needs.

That Imago Type of Love

What I've now come to realize is that when your emotional baggage gets kicked up in your relationship, it's not something to run away from but rather an opportunity for growth and healing.

There's a type of therapy called Imago. It was developed in the 1980s by the husband-and-wife team of Dr. Harville Hendrix and Dr. Helen LaKelly Hunt. It explores the idea of why we're hopelessly attracted to people who at the same time tend to trigger us. They believe that we enter romantic relationships as adults that bring up some of the same feelings we experienced in our childhood relationships. The partner you attract is essentially meant to help you heal your familial wounds, and vice versa. That's why conflict is actually an opportunity rather than a problem. It helps us deal with emotional baggage that we are better off letting go of in the long run.

But if you don't put forth the effort to work on that healing, you'll be stuck in a cycle of conflict and fighting that can lead to divorce.

I truly believe Kenny is my Imago guy and I'm his Imago gal. Together, we've helped each other heal from past conditioning and relationship programming that does not serve us. But that doesn't mean it didn't suck while we were doing it. And we are still doing it (we will likely help each other heal and grow for the rest of our lives).

As I started to require more of Kenny, he didn't like it because he didn't get to have as much freedom as before, and I didn't like it because I hated asking for extra help. I couldn't be the chill, easygoing girlfriend I had been because we had kids to care for. For the first few years of our marriage, I tried to keep that delicate, codependent balance stable, and dear Lord did I fail miserably.

Marriage and babies turned me into a woman I didn't recognize. I used to be fancy-free and adventurous. I felt like I had lost myself as a new mom. I had no idea how to crawl out of the hole I had created. What I realize now (but did not understand at the time) was that I was so unhappy because I wasn't advocating for my own needs. I was being the martyr mother.

Once, I attended a talk by Dr. Pat Allen, who is the author of *Getting to I Do*. I was twenty-six at the time, and she talked about how marriage and relationships were all about negotiation. I was surprised to hear that because it didn't line up with all the romantic comedies I had watched.

Now that I'm a grown-ass lady who's popped out two babies, I *really* know what the hell she was talking about—and it has nothing to do with romance. Men are socialized to be selfish. They're taught to ask for what they want, and they expect to get it. They make demands without apology and expect compliance.

Women, on the other hand, are socialized to be generous. We're taught to bend over backward, prioritize the needs of others, and not be "too much." Because of our respective programming, one-sided marriages are all too common.

I know so many women who are in unhappy marriages, and I'm sure you do too. Marriages where the wives are stuck at home taking care of the family while their husbands are out galivanting and living their best lives. And let's be real here, it's fucked up. Super fucked up, and we deserve better.

But guess what? There's no fairy godmother who's going to appear out of the sky and grant us our freedom back. Ain't nobody gonna save your trapped ass from your marriage, job, relationship, lack of health, or anything. It's up to you to save yourself. We're the only ones with the power to create equity in our lives. And the only way to do that is by taking action. You gotta have the tits to fight for what you deserve. There's no way around it.

Take the pay gap, for example. We know it sucks, and we can share meme after meme about it on social media, but that isn't going to do anything. You know what will? Going to YOUR boss and requesting a raise. The more women who do that, the smaller the gap will get.

So if I wanted the dynamic of my marriage to change, I had to be the one to change it. I had to make things fairer. One thing you'll learn throughout this book is that when women decide to lead, the world becomes a better, fairer place for them to exist in. The question is, what is it going to take for you to be willing to lead?

It took me getting to the point where I was so unbelievably unhappy and on the verge of divorce to finally begin to advocate for my needs and demand what I wanted. And when I say *demand*, I mean it. Not sure if you've noticed, but dudes will give you the shaft as long as you let them, so don't let them.

I'm sure the idea of fighting like a queen conjures up images of very still women with statue faces staying cool, calm, and collected as they head off to battle. But sometimes (especially in the beginning), fighting like a queen means being willing to be the biggest bitch in the room.

There were times when I would up and leave Kenny alone with the kids and go to my mom's for the weekend just to illustrate that I would no longer tolerate our dynamic. A word to the wise: When talking isn't effective, stop. Men often respond to actions more than words. So if you need to take action, do it.

The worst year in our entire marriage set the stage for the pivot to live happily ever after because we were willing to embrace the other side of Imago therapy: seeing conflict as an opportunity for growth and realizing that meeting our partner's needs was the blueprint for said growth.

That's right, sister, the first step in learning how to fight like a queen is to be willing to go to war on your own behalf. It might not come to that, but I want you to raise your level of commitment to self-honoring. If you do not honor yourself, no one else will honor you either. Your move.

Now Let's Fight

The divorce rate in America is insanely high. About 40–50 percent of marriages end in divorce, and the divorce rate for any subsequent marriage is even higher.[57]

Although I'm sure there are a lot of reasons for that, I believe a major one is the lack of education on how to resolve conflict when it rises, and it always inevitably arises. People seem to have a negative impression of conflict. I've had clients say, "Oh, me and my husband are fighting. I think I would be better off alone." Or "Oh, me and my husband are fighting. This must mean that we shouldn't be together."

We've been programmed to believe that conflict means there is something "wrong."

What Imago therapy teaches is that conflict is just change trying to happen. It's just like when you grow a baby in your belly, your skin stretches and your organs get squished because this baby is growing in there and creating pressure. And let's not forget about how completely painful and improper the birthing process is. This is the miracle of life we are talking about, and that shit ain't pretty.

So we seem to have this misconception that conflict is bad, when in fact it's just the natural tension, pain, and suffering that happens when growth and miracles occur.

If your relationship harbors an unhealthy dynamic, then conflict is an opportunity to change that. When things are looking bad, uncomfortable, or like the end is near, it's really an invitation to grow and expand into the next evolution of your relationship. You can transfer this idea to your life, business, philosophy, level of health, career, or anything, for that matter, where you feel the rumbling of change. It's always darkest before dawn, and my darkest moments have paved the way for me to make the transition from people-pleasing zombie to revolutionary woman.

This theory of conflict resolution does not apply to relationships where domestic abuse or sexual violence is present. Many people use bullying as a means of exerting power and control, and that's abuse. If that's happening to you, you need to seek help immediately and get the fuck out. Your life is too valuable and precious to be tormented and tortured like that. Oh hell no.

But for those of you who are struggling to see eye to eye with your partners about helping out more with the kids, being more romantic, or getting on the same page financially—a little fighting is par for the course.

I spent the first few years of my marriage realizing that our dynamic was not the healthiest. My inner rebel was slowly waking up (and building tons of resentment in the process) until year five, when I couldn't hold it in anymore and revolted against the system I had co-created.

I was so fed up with how we were operating that I constantly picked fights, acted ragey, and threatened divorce. It was a really ugly time full of outbursts and uncomfortable silences. He would breathe wrong and

I would freak the fuck out. It wasn't fun, but it was a necessary learning curve for me. I was learning to go from being a people-pleasing yes-woman to a self-expressing queen. It's just that when you are learning a new skill you often swing to the other side of the pendulum, and so I swung, and I swung hard.

Luckily, I am blessed with a badass man who was able to withstand my Old World Middle Eastern rage (he is after all the mighty Thor). But this was a necessary step for us to have longevity in our relationship. It paved the way for our new normal. I was learning how to speak up, and as you know sometimes when you learn, you fuck up royally in the process.

When we were in couple's therapy (get the support of a neutral third party; I don't know how marriages last without it), our therapist would constantly commend us for showing up even through the fighting. She said so many marriages end because people sweep things under the rug. She called it death by a thousand papercuts.

It's a slow process in which a myriad of small, seemingly insignificant wrongs occur that never get addressed, and they lead to the demise of what we once viewed as our one true love. She commended us for being willing to fight at the five-year mark in our marriage so that we weren't dead by the ten-year mark. Not fighting, it seems, leads to divorce much more than fighting does. Do you see how we had it backward?

At the time of this book's release, Kenny and I have been together for over a decade. And I'd like to assure you that we have a much healthier, happier relationship than we did before. It seems fighting was productive. The old dynamic of me sacrificing myself for him and the kids to get what they wanted at my expense is dead (thank God). The new dynamic where I honor myself, advocate for my needs, prioritize my health and happiness just as much as any other member of the family is the new normal. And may I just say that it is glorious.

I'll give you an example of how we changed it. Not too long ago, Kenny told me that a new video game was coming out, and he wanted to spend the whole weekend playing it. Which means I would basically have to play single mom all weekend. Old Shereenie would have been like, "Oh, that's cool, babe, go for it," and then would have retroactively felt resentful at my lack of freedom in comparison to his. But I've learned. New Shereenie responded with, "That sounds good, babe. What are you going to give me?"

Although advocating for my needs was very dramatic in the beginning (because speaking up was super scary to my inner codependent), it's not like that anymore. It's just a simple conversation, or a healthy negotiation. Today, all I do is make sure that I'm inserting myself into the equation. I'm making sure that I am not a yes-woman, and this is not the Kenny and the Kids Show. But it was up to me to make that internal shift to express my desires and get my needs met, just like it's up to you. This is what I mean when I say we can take back our power at any moment, but it's up to us to do it.

It isn't your fault that the systemic disempowerment of women left us with tons of mind trash to heal. But it *is* your responsibility to heal it. No one can do that for you. In this matrix, you are the one.

One way you can start to implement this is by taking a moment before committing to something. Just take a breath and think for a second about how it will affect you and your life. Consider your own needs before you say yes. Question whether you're going to regret saying yes and resent the person for "making" you do this. Because guess what? No one makes you do anything. You are responsible for your life, so handle that responsibility with care. You deserve it.

Six Steps to Healthy Conflict Resolution

Now that you see that conflict isn't "bad" but rather a beautiful opportunity that leads to healing and growth, it's time to learn how to handle it when it arises. Queen style.

Whether you're feeling the tension in your romantic, platonic, or professional relationship, the first thing you must do is address it. Don't let hurt feelings or miscommunications fester. The longer they do, the more complicated and supercharged the situation will feel.

When we let people sit in our uncomfortable silence—be it across the room or with a text left without a reply—we give them permission to create their own stories. They'll decide what it was we *really* meant or how we're *actually* feeling about something they did. In this space, they bring their own projections and traumas to heighten a conflict that could be resolved through some simple clarifying communication.

Yes, it's their shit they're putting on you. But by not responding or by leaving something unsaid, you allowed that space of projections to exist. To fight like a queen, you have to take responsibility for how a conflict will be resolved. And despite what "they" say, time does not heal all wounds—especially if the person who stabbed you refuses to pick up your call and talk about it.

Now that we've agreed that actively participating in a conflict is the only way to resolve it, it's time to go over some of my most effective strategies for fighting fair even when you're royally pissed off.

1. Ask for Permission.
Conflict is not a casual endeavor, so it's best to ask for permission to discuss it. This may feel formal and awkward, but it sets the context for respect and courtesy while engaging in conflict resolution. If you randomly hit someone with an "I feel" statement out of the blue, they may be way too stressed out from work to deal with it. They may have explosive diarrhea. They may have a myriad of reasons why they would give you a less-than-ideal response to your vulnerability. For this reason, it's wise to check in with them and see if they have the proper bandwidth for the discussion. If yes, proceed, and if no, let them know you want to resolve a conflict with them and make an appointment to do so. This could sound

like, "I hear that now is not a good time. Is there a time that might work better for you?"

It's that simple. Don't force yourself onto someone, but also don't allow yourself to be blown off. It's always up to you to get your needs met, so go get it, girl.

2. Come with The Good Vibes.

When both parties are engaging in a consensual conflict resolution, the party has officially started. I'm proud of you already. So, what kind of energy do you bring to the party? Good energy! Don't be a downer and act like it's a dark day; the fact that you both care about each other enough to show up speaks volumes about your love and care for one another. That is grounds for celebration in and of itself.

So don't go into it with your fists clenched and claws out. Remember you are a leader, and it's up to you to bring an optimal attitude to the situation. If you believe that you are right and they are wrong, then, honey, you are not ready to talk.

Take a beat and vent to a friend, a coach, or a therapist (because when we are triggered, we be crazy). I suggest a neutral third party rather than a friend if it's about your intimate partner because friends can get very protective of you and accidentally add fuel to the fire. This can further complicate your life because now you have too many fucking fires to put out.

In a safe space with a neutral third party, you can get clarity on what you really want underneath all the triggers so that when you engage in resolving the conflict you are actually ready to fight fair. This sets you up to come into the discussion viewing the other party as a well-intended human being who likely had no ill will. In that head space you are much more likely to be open-minded and seek to understand rather than trying to make them wrong.

The energy of conflict resolution is grounded, calm, wise, and fair. It doesn't have an obsession with being right. In life you either get to be right or you get to be happy, but you don't get both. Bring your good vibes and your emotional maturity so that you can be present to address tender emotions.

3. Set the Context.

Before engaging in what the conflict is about, share how you would like to communicate throughout this conversation and have them share that with you too. So, before you engage, you are basically agreeing on *how* you want to engage. This may seem extra extra formal, but again we are trying to mitigate explosions here, darling. According to the SCARF model, conflict can be perceived by the brain as physical danger, so we are just doing our best to help you create resolution rather than explosions.[58]

You could say something like, "I know conflict can sometimes feel scary and emotions can get heightened ... so before we talk, I'd love for us to talk through how we both want to engage."

If they agree to it, then you can ask them, "What would you like me to keep in mind while we talk about this?"

Now it's your turn to listen. Then you can share what's important to you, too. I might say something like:

1. It's important to me that we both feel heard.
2. It's important to me that we operate from a place of mutual respect.
3. It's important to me that we resolve this fully, that is, this ends in an apology, forgiveness, and a plan on how we can honor each other more in the future.
4. It's important to me that we learn from this experience and view it in a positive light.

This also gets both parties into a place of agreement. As you agree with each other on how you want to communicate, it strengthens your rapport and creates a "yes energy" between you two that makes it easier to arrive at a place of resolution as you embark on discussing the more sensitive topic.

4. Don't Play the Blame Game.

Just as we don't want the other person making assumptions, we, too, have to put our blame to the side. We have to go into the conflict resolution conversation with the understanding that no one else is responsible for our happiness and how we feel. No one *makes* us feel a certain way. And no one is a mind reader. If the other person has no idea what is bothering you or what you want, you can't expect them to do anything about it.

Seek to take responsibility for how you co-created this issue. It wasn't until I took responsibility for how I was acting like a yes-woman that I was able to see how I co-created a one-sided marriage. It wasn't his fault. We were two imperfect humans who took the shit we learned from our families of origin into our romantic relationship, which is pretty typical. No one was the villain, and no one was the victim. We were two consenting adults who were renegotiating our relationship agreements.

To be productive in resolving conflict, you must not play the blame game. Focus on sharing how you feel. Communicate what your expectations are. Be honest about what you want moving forward and what you truly desire.

So many of us avoid conflict because we have often felt attacked, defensive, misunderstood, and abandoned. When we start off the conversation with "I" statements instead of "you" statements, the other person is more likely to lower their guard and be more receptive to what we have to say. They get the opportunity to feel empathy for your feelings rather than feeling attacked. Don't forget you are a leader, and you have the ability to lead the climate of the conversation.

An example of this would sound similar to the boundaries conversation we reviewed in the last chapter:

> "I feel hurt when I don't get alone time with you because I feel unimportant. What I need is for us to have a weekly date night so that alone time happens more frequently."

This way the person understands how you feel and what you want rather than feeling criticized.

5. Check for Understanding.

Once you've said your initial piece, have them share what they heard you say. This will allow you to check for any communication mishaps (and there are often many). So, again, though this may seem like an extra-formal step, it's very necessary because communication can be very complex.

Once you feel understood, it is your turn to listen. Agree before the conversation even starts to not interrupt each other and to listen actively (when you're setting the context). Don't come up with responses in your head while they are talking, just take in what they're saying.

When the other person is finished talking, repeat back what you believe they said. This will give them a chance to feel heard and clear up any misunderstandings. So many of our conflicts are based on assumptions and projections (I could write an entirely different book about that). It's up to us to make sure we get clarity on what's really going on. Otherwise, we'll just keep spinning in circles and repeating past trauma without resolving it and moving forward.

Once you feel like you've got a good grasp of their perspective, ask them if they're open to a response. If they are, carefully lay out your thoughts. Again, do this using "I" statements and with the emphasis on resolution—not picking at old wounds. It's okay to make sure the person knows you were hurt by something they did, but harping on it doesn't do anyone any good. You can either accept an apology and choose to move forward together, or you can decide that you no longer want to participate in a relationship that feels toxic.

This structured way of speaking is a far cry from how we usually fight. Because of that, it might feel awkward and even a bit forced. If you can't help but slip into old fighting patterns like yelling and name-calling, it might help to call in a third party. Having a counselor, pastor, coach, or mediator present can be a great way to ease into this queen-like style of fighting fair. It's also a great way to get the support you need to *make sure you are heard* in your relationships.

As I mentioned, I am certified in conflict mediation, and I can tell you firsthand that just the presence of a neutral third party gets everyone to put their bad behavior in check. This makes for a much safer environment for you to express yourself and make progress.

6. Make a Plan.

Once both sides have had a chance to speak and be heard, it's time to come up with a plan for resolution. We leave so many fights without this and doing so just invites us to come back to those same old arguments again and again.

The only way to break negative patterns is to have preventative plans in place. For example, let's say you and your partner are fighting because you feel like they have more free time than you do. You're taking care of the kids and working, and somehow, they have time to go golfing and hit the gym.

By the end of your conversation, you both need to come up with a plan you can agree on so that you both feel like you have an equal amount of personal time. Maybe that looks like agreeing on different days of the week when one of you gets to work out or take a few hours to yourself while the other handles the household duties. Maybe it's them sacrificing one of their nights out so that you can meet up with your friends for a drink. Maybe it's budgeting some extra money for a babysitter so you can both have a moment alone.

Whatever the resolution is, you should both walk away with an agreement that honors you and that you can realistically stick to. It also helps to check in on said plan a week or two later to see if it's working or if it needs a bit of updating. This prevents future conflicts from arising.

So there you have it. That's my Six Steps to Healthy Conflict Resolution, and I hope it supports you.

Up-Level Your Leadership

I stress the importance of healthy conflict in relationships (romantic and platonic) because I see the implications of having a nation of human beings running around too afraid to deal with uncomfortable feels. Sexism. Racism. Prejudice. Toxic relationships. People hate to bring these things up because we're more comfortable pretending it's not happening. But it is, and it needs to be addressed so that change can occur.

But while you're wading through the struggle of growth, I want to remind you to have faith. During that crazy year of learning how to do conflict in my marriage, I eventually calmed down from my Old World Middle Eastern rage and decided I wasn't going to fight at the expense of my own peace of mind (not only was I making Kenny crazy, but I was making myself crazy too).

And you know what? I got more of what I wanted from Kenny when I calmed down.

Even though sometimes you gotta let shit out and have the courage to fight for what you want, you also have to get calm enough to communicate effectively. This is why working your shit out with a coach or counselor beforehand can be helpful so that you aren't dumping it all into the conflict resolution conversation. You are changing, and you are up-leveling the way you relate to yourself and to the world, so get yourself the support you need.

One of my favorite Martin Luther King Jr. quotes sums it up best: "The ultimate measure of a (wo)man is not where (s)he stands in moments of comfort and convenience, but where (s)he stands at times of challenge and controversy."

I want you to first have the courage to create the controversy in the name of what is right, fair, just, and equal. And then I want you to up-level your leadership so that you can fight fair and stay in integrity with who you truly are.

The soul knows truth. The soul speaks truth. And the soul does not cower in the face of conflict. Sometimes it needs to get real bad before it gets real good. And we all need to be a little more willing to surrender to all the phases and stages of life. The good, the bad, and the ugly.

You want to know the craziest thing about all of this? Kenny did not fucking change. I'm the only one who changed. My mindset shift is the only thing that course-corrected our marriage and got us into a healthier dynamic. When you change, the people around you inevitably adjust to the change or they leave. It's just physics. So what I'm saying here is that you don't need permission from anyone to make changes. You just need to get real with yourself about the quality of life, relationships, career, and health you want and accept nothing less.

That's why women's empowerment is not only an important but also a necessary aspect of healing a nation. We have the power to set the tone for how things go. Once we set the tone that our needs are a priority, everyone will follow our lead and we will live in a fairer and more equitable world.

— Life Work —

Now let's set you up to fight like a queen by doing some of the suggested exercises in this chapter.

1. Grab a pen and a journal and answer these questions:
    a. Who are the primary relationships in your life?
        i. What are the unspoken agreements you have with them?
        ii. How do these unspoken agreements make you feel?
        iii. Do you want to continue with these agreements or make updates?
            1. If so, do you need to engage in any conflict resolution efforts or boundary setting chats to clarify these updates with anyone?
        iv. What agreements do you want to make with yourself that will support you in optimal health and happiness?

7
FUCK UP
Royally

*Sometimes we fall down because there's something
down there we have to find.*
—Unknown

*I*n an ideal world, the biggest hurdle we would ever have to face is figuring out what our purpose is. Once we realize what it is we're supposed to be doing on this rotating ball floating in space, everything should just fall into place, right?

Not exactly.

The most troubling part about living as your authentic self lies within the gap of where you are now and where you want to be. You have to be willing to navigate uncertainty, gamble with outcomes, and persevere when things don't go according to plan.

And trust me—they never do. Knowing what you want to do isn't nearly the same thing as actually going out and doing it. I wish it were easier, but figuring out your purpose is actually where the journey begins. As modern-day humans, we've grown very accustomed to being comfortable. Between apps that deliver our groceries and binge-able TV shows at the push of a button, we're programmed to expect instant gratification with just about everything.

Although that may work for Chinese takeout, no app will fast-track you to living the life of your dreams (I should try to create one though lol). If you want to fulfill your purpose, getting comfortable with uncertainty and learning how to move through fear are crucial skills.

Recent research from Yale found that the feeling of uncertainty actually triggers our brain to start learning new information.[59] Another study found that being in new places and experiencing new things releases dopamine, the happy chemical, in our brain.[60] Both of these findings point to the benefits of having a growth mindset versus a fixed one.

When we have a growth mindset, our brains support ongoing learning, which helps us feel happier and more successful. We're not afraid to trip up or make mistakes because we know eventually we'll get it.

A fixed mindset, on the other hand, keeps us stuck. We feel stupid for trying anything new, so we avoid being beginners. When we have a fixed mindset, we're so terrified of failure that we never even try to go after our dreams. Even if we do, all it takes is one off-hand comment or slight slip-up to send us running back to our comfort zone with our tail between our legs.

But failure, my darling, is your salvation. I know this because I've failed. I've failed gloriously.

I failed all the way to my purpose. I failed all the way to my soulmate. I failed all the way to my happiness. And—in a super weird-ass way—my failures turned into my greatest accomplishments.

You see, when you have a greater willingness to fail, you're more likely to be able to see the lessons you're meant to learn. You can spot the ways you're resisting so that you can stop, course-correct, and get back into the flow of life.

Another of my favorite Maya Angelou quotes is, "Courage allows the successful woman to fail and learn powerful lessons from the failure. So that in the end, she didn't fail at all."

What I've learned is that often what you'll find in moments of "failure" is courage and strength that you never knew you had.

We've been told repeatedly that failure, pain, conflict, discomfort, and pretty much every other negative emotion is a signal that something is wrong. But that couldn't be further from the truth.

So we're going to rewrite the script on what it means to fail and learn how to see failure as something to embrace with open arms—and maybe even a shot of whiskey.

The Great Experiment

You may have a long-buried dream that you know deep down in your soul you're meant to chase. Or you may have no idea what you want to do—you just know what you're doing right now ain't it.

If the latter situation describes you, congratulations. You just became a scientist, and your purpose is your next great experiment.

In coaching, we call this the "reshuffling phase." It's that period in your life when you're not sure what you're doing, but you know you need to shake it up to get on the right track. Sometimes you throw shit at the wall to see what sticks; sometimes you pivot entirely. But the key is that you are willing to navigate the uncertainty in order to get to the other side.

This can be such an exciting place to be if you don't fight it the whole way through. Remember that whole bit about how suffering is optional? You get to choose your attitude about it. And if you choose wisely, you're more likely to discover your yellow brick road when you're relaxed and able to see the signs. Coming from a place of curiosity will be more effective than attempting to force an outcome.

You can't get clarity and tune in to your inner knowing without first accepting that, at this moment, you don't know. And that's okay.

Even if you do have some clarity on what you want to do, you still don't know how you're going to make it all work. So no matter what, you have to be willing to go through this completely necessary (and occasionally annoying) phase.

There will be mistakes.

There will be dead ends.

There will be totally embarrassing falling-flat-on-your-face moments.

And you will come out the other side with an unmatched sense of clarity, purpose, and drive. Not to mention some amazing stories.

It's Never Too Late

I want to remind you that it's never too late to go through your reshuffling phase. In fact, many of my clients have not only gone through theirs later in life—but also gone through it multiple times. Each time they do, it gets a little easier (and a little more fun—and that's "fun" as in it's less scary as you get used to the fact that this is just part of life. So, it's still scary, but it's also exciting).

Society loves to make us feel like we're only of value to the world when we're young, hot, rich, or famous. But part of awakening your rebel and becoming a revolutionary woman is staring those super shallow, incorrect standards in the face and kindly telling them to fuck off.

You have the power to decide what each phase of your life is going to look like. And, honestly, we have much more ability, skill, and knowledge to make incredible changes the more experience and self-assuredness we have.

Reshuffling is a long-term skill that, when developed, can make your life richer and more successful than you can ever imagine. So please don't see this book (or your life) as a one-and-done kind of project. Just like you, the expression of your purpose is ever changing. You will always be anchored to the Life Purpose Statement you created for yourself, but the expression of that purpose will evolve. And isn't that the beauty of it?

I started learning how to reshuffle in my late twenties, and then did it again in my thirties. And even now, I'm still reshuffling what I want my life to look like as a mom, a business owner, an adventurer, a freedom lover, and a creative soul. I just recently decided to honor the part of me that wants to learn to fly a plane. Wildly illogical and unnecessary (allegedly), but my soul knows that it's my next great adventure. And why the fuck not?!

Stand-up comedy was ages ago, and I get to have adventures in my life so long as I am alive and kicking. That's the life I choose for me, and I know that I am the captain of my ship (or the pilot of my plane). This is how I choose to live this one beautiful God-given gift we call life. To honor my inner desires and trust that my soul doesn't lead me astray. To say yes to myself instead of saying no. To allow myself to truly live.

Things are constantly changing, and there's no need to get caught up in what you should and shouldn't be doing just because you became a mom, reached a certain age, went broke, or had a breakup. You can make your life whatever you want it to be at any time. Do you, booboo!

My First Time

I can't mention the hilarious stories that are born out of this reshuffling phase and fear of failure without telling you the story of my first time trying stand-up comedy. It's the scariest thing I've ever done.

Remember that seminar I went to that I mentioned before? Well, it was that weekend that I made the commitment to say the ultimate YES to myself and finally try comedy. I quit that obligatory master's degree program and set the goal to do comedy three times in three months.

I was equal parts ecstatic and terrified. I signed up at a local open mic and was number twenty on the list. When they finally called my name, I knew it was time to get up and do it.

While this is a fun story to hear, there is purpose in me sharing it, so pay attention. I want to illustrate what we are up against when our brains perceive a threat, fear, or failure.

This was the scariest thing I had ever attempted in my entire life, and still is to this day. I have jumped out of planes, gone into labor without an epidural, and started a business with no safety net—but doing stand-up for the first time remains number one on my list of scariest things I've ever done. So, it's the perfect story to illustrate what happens when we face fear.

Most of the fear gripped me during the fifteen seconds it took me to rise from my seat, walk onto the stage, and grab the microphone. It all happened very fast, and as I type these words over a decade later, I feel my heart race in remembrance of this insane moment in time.

My brain went fucking nuts. It started trying to convince me to leave, to hide, to run, to dodge, to do anything to avoid the perceived humiliation I was inevitably about to experience.

These are the thoughts that raced through my head in those fifteen seconds:
You're such a fucking idiot.
You're about to look so stupid.
This was a terrible idea!
You can still run out the door! Leave!

To be honest, they weren't clear, separate thoughts like I've listed them here. It was more like a panicked voice screaming them all at once as rapidly as possible. I looked at the door to see if I could make an escape as my brain pleaded with me to get the fuck out of there.

It was really intense. But I headed to the stage. I put one foot in front of the other as my brain screamed and raged against this wildly frightening thing I was about to do, and then I grabbed that fucking mic.

The actual five minutes onstage was fun. I started my set and lost myself a bit, rambling on about some embarrassingly personal stories. Then got back on track. There were times people laughed, and sometimes my jokes didn't hit, and just as quickly as it started, my mission was complete. I had officially done stand-up comedy for the first time.

I had written jokes, signed up, got onstage, shared some shenanigans—and I left that stage forever changed.

Your Brain on Drugs

The question is, Why was my brain screaming at me?

If this was something that was the start to me revolutionizing my life and prioritizing my true desires, why did my brain want to stop me?

Well, our brains are basically wired to keep us safe. The amygdala, two tiny parts buried deep in the cerebrum that are responsible for emotional processing among other things, gets your body ready to react to a potential threat or dangerous situation in order to protect you.[61] Although that worked wonders for our ancestors who were fighting off wild animals, it doesn't work so well for us when we're trying something new or navigating uncertainty in the modern world.

As you can see, my brain worked overtime trying to save me from that new experience, which it perceived as a fatal threat. But, knowing the threat was not real, I did what all of us must do: I did it anyway.

And you know what? It wasn't that bad. I was decently funny for a first-timer, but that wasn't what mattered. What mattered was the message I sent to my unconscious mind that day.

"What you want matters. You can trust your inspiration. You are brave. You can overcome fear and live a wildly exciting life that's worthy of you. I hear you, I see you, I honor you. And we get to have so much fun!"

You see, it's not so much about the "thing" we're so afraid of doing. It doesn't matter if it's stand-up comedy, asking out the hot barista, or running a marathon. It's about taking action that proves to your subconscious mind that you are no longer ruled by fear. You're telling that deep-rooted part of your brain that thinks you can't that you *can*. You're rewriting mindset limitations that have kept you small in your life.

Remember that patriarchal voice I mentioned in the Introduction? The one that commands all women to stay small? When you trust your desires and face your fears, you are minimizing that voice and raising your self-esteem.

Step by step, scary action by scary action, our subconscious mind catches up and starts operating from a place of power rather than of fear.

But don't think it won't try to sabotage you in the process.

Don't Back Down

Because we are all wired to want to belong and fit in with our families and communities, experimenting with different, better ways of living our lives brings up a lot of shit.

As you're trying new things, you're simultaneously reprogramming your brain to get rid of old beliefs and adopt new ones. It's a far more complex process than it sounds.

Basically, it goes like this.

Sally decides she wants to run a 5K. So, she finds a training program, buys some new shoes, and plans to run after work. The workday ends, but instead of running, she meets her buddies for happy hour at a local brewery.

Slightly annoyed with herself, she makes another commitment to run after work the next day. This time she goes, but she hasn't run in ten years, so after a quarter of a mile, she's totally out of breath. Angry with her out-of-shape body, she stops her run before it's over and heads home.

A week later, Sally reads an article about a girl like her who hadn't run in a while and was finally able to run a 5K. She creates a new training schedule and decides to run in the morning instead of after work. This time, she makes it a full mile before stopping.

Our pal Sally will hit these highs and lows again and again until she reaches her 5K goal. She'll have twenty different running schedules, four new pairs of shoes, a scraped knee, and a penchant for cottonmouth before she reaches her goal.

Why? Because she's got to mentally transform the way she's thought about running for the past ten years. It's no surprise that doesn't happen overnight. It's not about the running, it's about the mindset.

Success and sustainable change are not linear. There's a lot of experimenting and tweaking that need to happen along the way. And most of that fine-tuning is a result of deprogramming whatever old beliefs you've had on the subject and finding new ones.

As luck would have it, it's much easier to stay on course when you're aware of what those old beliefs are.

Just Get Up

The best piece of advice I ever got was from a fellow stand-up comic, who told me that the first time onstage was not about being funny. It was just about getting up.

Just like the example with Sally and her dream of running a 5K, my experience with stand-up shows us that it doesn't matter *how* we do it. It just matters *that* we do it.

It doesn't matter if you mess up. It doesn't matter if you miss the workout or the article doesn't go viral. All you have to do is be open to tweaks and be willing to show up and try and try again.

If you're committed to a dream, and you keep going, pivoting as necessary, then you are on the right path. And it's actually a lot more fun to chase a goal when we leave room for surprise.

This mindset seriously took the pressure off of my first time doing comedy, and I hope that it can do the same for all of the firsts you are about to embark upon.

The Loser Leader

To go where you've never gone before, you have to be cool with being a beginner. That means not killing it the first time. Not having all the answers. Not looking like a total badass when you're out doing whatever it is you want to do.

Getting comfortable with uncertainty means letting your inner loser run the show for a while (you know you want to). And when the version of yourself that's a total dweeb is in charge, you'll finally get to let go of

- The need to look good
- The need to be right
- Fear of looking stupid

Because here's the deal: You get to be right, or you get to be happy. You don't get to have both. You have to be willing to feel the fear of looking stupid and do it anyway. You have to be willing to let people find out that you're not a total genius and move forward anyway. You have to be willing to get it wrong a couple of times and keep going anyway.

That is how you become superhuman—by not giving a fuck. By putting your ego in check so that there is room for exploration, play, and learning.

It's something I've learned over the course of my life, and it's really helped me become more honest and vulnerable—especially in those moments when I had to embrace being a beginner.

So, please, if you take absolutely nothing else from this book, take this: Give yourself permission to fuck up royally. Allow yourself to be disappointed, embarrassed, and a little hurt, and still show up the next day. Call in the part of you that doesn't need to be perfect because she isn't looking for approval, she's looking to truly live. That will give you space to fail, experiment, and, ultimately, find your way.

— Life Work —

Grab your journal and a pen and write down all of your irrational impulses. All your bucket list shit. Anything and everything that you want to do but historically have talked yourself out of.

Be specific or be vague, but just give yourself the gift of freedom in this moment to not "make sense" or "be responsible." Just be the truth, and give yourself permission to look dumb, to be crazy, and to fuck up royally. Remember, this is the phase where uncertainty is not only fine but also encouraged.

Once you've got your list, write a list of all the reasons it's "not okay" for you to embark upon these desires. Keep this list somewhere handy. Because when obstacles arise—and they will—you'll want to look at the list to see which belief is being activated.

Next, write a list of all the ways embarking upon these adventures will change your life. And keep this list even closer because it holds the secrets your soul keeps about why these are actually the best things you can possibly do.

Keep in mind that doing stand-up comedy was something that I could have reasonably talked myself out of. It won't make me any money, it will be hard, I will look stupid, and the list goes on. But I had the desire, and so I did it anyway. What I didn't know at the time was that this choice would be the catalyst for me building an entire brand and a lifelong career after the fact.

I want you to think about that as your rational mind kicks in to talk you out of what your soul desires. You never know which of your irrational and frivolous impulses will actually lead you to your soul's true purpose.

8

DESIGN Like a Boss

The opposite of love is indifference,
and the opposite of happiness is boredom.
—Timothy Ferriss

*I*f you've been operating on societal and familial cruise control for most of your life, the idea that you can curate a lifestyle by your design may seem strange and downright unrealistic. But the truth of the matter is, you've been doing it this whole time; you just never realized it.

Every decision you have made—from what you had for breakfast twenty years ago to who you have dated—has led you to where you are now. Although that may infuriate you if your circumstances aren't favorable, it should also empower you because you have the power to design something entirely new.

You are always one decision away from a completely different life. We know this, and yet we still make the same old safe choices over and over again that keep us feeling stuck inside. No judgment, girlfriend, I've done this tons.

Why do we do it? As it turns out, we do about 99.9 percent of our decision-making using our brains. We put our faith in logic and common sense when we make the choices that ultimately shape our lives.

I, like you, have spent much of my time here on earth making sensible decisions. I've based my next steps on things like money, my reputation, social acceptance, and whether or not I would be exposing myself to emotional distress by means of failure.

The "right" decision was always:

A. Realistic

B. Financially sound

C. Deemed "okay" by society or my parents

However, the "right" decision never made me happy. Even if I felt like I was a successful human, that moment of success was fleeting. And once it was gone, I was left feeling like yet again I had sacrificed a part of my soul to fit into some mold that I didn't even like.

So why do we make decisions that are fundamentally opposite to what will make us happy? Decisions that sometimes even get in the way of our happiness?

Even though research shows that we make decisions using both cognition *and* emotion, as individuals we tend to lean toward one or the other decision-making practice.[62] It's no surprise that most of us (a whopping 79 percent) use our head to make decisions.

However, those who more closely followed their heart (especially in terms of their career) were more likely to be satisfied.

Although making decisions based on logic may seem like the right thing to do, remember that in the long run you're the one who will suffer the most if you ignore your heart.

Which is why the only move to make is to design a life you love with all your heart. And lucky for you, I have the formula to help you do just that. But before we explore my formula for Lifestyle Design, let's look at some Old World wisdom.

Finding Your Ikigai

The Japanese concept of *ikigai* literally means your "reason for being."

It's the convergence of four different elements that, when brought together, form your ikigai and, therefore, help you create a meaningful direction for your life.

Following are the four elements:
- **Your passion:** What you love
- **Your mission:** What the world needs
- **Your vocation:** What you are good at
- **Your profession:** What you can get paid for

When you use those four elements to determine your ikigai, you learn how to turn the things you love into a way to serve the world *and* create the lifestyle you want.

Yes, following your ikigai can lead to success and a badass life. But it can also bring your life meaning and purpose right now, without having to achieve anything. When you know you're on a path you care deeply about, living in a way that honors your soul, the gas in your tank never runs out.

Research has shown that people who live in Blue Zones—aka regions of the world where people are happiest and live the longest with the least amount of disease—all practice some version of ikigai. One eleven-year study of these zones found that people between the ages of sixty-five and ninety-two who had a strong sense of purpose were less likely to suffer from Alzheimer's disease, arthritis, and stroke.[63]

So, yes, discovering your purpose, or your ikigai, will not only make you happier but also help you live a healthier, longer life.

Comedian-Turned-Coach

After my first time onstage, I was hooked. I felt like I had finally found my path and would pursue a full-time career in entertainment—something that I had felt called to do ever since I was a little girl. Back then, all I wanted was a big entertainment career. Singer, dancer, professional athlete—it didn't matter so long as I was doing it big.

Stand-up comedy felt like the perfect home, so I did it for two years straight, and I did it hard. I drove to gigs in horrendous traffic, stayed up late, hung out at comedy clubs, networked my ass off, got onstage two to three times a week, and competed in comedy contests until one day a scout from MTV finally approached me after a show at the Hollywood Improv. It was always a goal of mine to be on TV, and MTV was at the top of my list. I was ecstatic. It was all going swimmingly, so everything after that should have been easy, right?

Wrong.

Just about the time when I got scouted, after two years of chasing this dream of a big entertainment career, I started to feel like it wasn't my dream anymore. I liked stand-up, but I hated the lifestyle that went with it. I'm a morning person, a closeted nerd. I might have a personality that comes off as the life of the party, but deep down I'm actually quite introverted.

I hated staying up late, and I didn't want to succeed in this industry only to have to become a road comic. I like to come and go as I please. I didn't want to spend New Year's Eve entertaining others; I wanted to kick it with my friends and family.

So, although I enjoyed making people laugh, the lifestyle aspects of this career were not a fit. I wasn't feeling it anymore. I began to care less whether I made people laugh from the stage, and I didn't want to waste the gas money on the drive. This was very confusing for me because I thought I had found my dream path.

Now, during the two years of comedy, I was simultaneously studying personal development. After attending that first seminar, I continued reading the books, going on the retreats, meeting with a coach, and revolutionizing my life. Having a coach is what gave me the courage to remove the mask of who I was "supposed to be" and start sharing my authentic self. This transformation gave me so much joy and energy, and it returned me to my essence. I felt so lit up by the idea of supporting others in this transformation as well, so I wanted to pay it forward.

For months, I struggled to make a choice. Sticking with comedy made so much sense in my head, especially because I had only been at it for two years and I was already getting scouted by big networks.

I sought advice from a seasoned and successful comedian, explaining to him what I was experiencing. I said, "What's wrong with me? Why don't I love comedy anymore? I'm actually starting to hate it."

And he replied, "That means you're about to get really good."

He was encouraging me to stick with it, but I knew I needed to let it go. I didn't want to be a miserable comic. I wanted to be a happy coach. So, despite my head telling me to stick with comedy because of the extrinsic rewards, I decided to listen to my heart and go all-in on coaching.

Your Revolutionary Life Formula

Even with coaching I had to figure out the business model that would match my desired lifestyle. I used the concept of ikigai but simplified it to create my version, which I call the Revolutionary Life Formula. It has three elements:

- **What you love:** What lights you up, what gets you excited, what feels fun to you

- **Your desired lifestyle:** What gives you the time freedom, income generation, and creative expression you desire
- **Your impact:** What impact you want to make, what purpose you want to serve, and what helps you avoid the number one regret of the dying (that is, what helps you live true to yourself rather than living the life other people expect of you)

That's it. Don't overthink it. That. Is. It.

Here's how it shook out for me in the brainstorming portion:

- **What I love:** Coaching, Entertaining, Speaking, Traveling, Being outdoors, Retreats, Comedy, Hosting, Being active, Dancing, Playing soccer, Connecting with amazing human beings, Live events, Talking deep & waxing poetic, Creativity, and Entrepreneurship
- **My desired lifestyle:** I want total time freedom, total control of my schedule, to be my own boss, to have infinite income generation potential, and to feel totally authentic while I'm doing it. I don't want to be bought or sold for a paycheck. I want to feel truly alive in my life, whether I'm working or playing. I want to be fully expressed as a writer, a comedian, a healer, and an adventurer.
- **My impact:** I want to empower women and people of color, I want to create a more equitable world, I want justice and peace, I want to be a force for healing old wounds and transmuting them into love, I want my children to be proud of me, and I want for them to feel empowered in their lives as a result of me choosing empowered living.

Here's how that informed my personal Revolutionary Life Formula:

- **What I love (and how that informs the way I do my work):** I created a creative entrepreneurial lifestyle brand via shereenthor.com that holds space for all of the things that I love. I am a host of a podcast, an author, and a coach.

- **My desired lifestyle:** I am my own boss and have a few different streams of income that allow me time freedom and total control over my schedule. I have infinite income generation potential, and I feel truly alive in my life whether I'm working or playing. This book changes lives while simultaneously giving me freedom. I offer Revolutionary Woman retreats where we do a digital detox which makes my work feel like play. I have a team that helps me, so that I can stay in my zone of genius (more on that below).
- **My impact:** My work empowers women and people of color every day. It is one hundred percent aligned with my values, makes a difference, and hopefully the kiddos will approve.

It took me about a decade and much trial and error to gain clarity on all of these items, but it doesn't have to take you as long. That is the purpose of this book: to share what I've learned so that it's easier and faster for you to implement this hard-won wisdom.

And now, my friend, it's your turn. I want you to spend some time brainstorming the three elements of your Revolutionary Life Formula.

Trust me when I say that you'll enjoy it more if you approach Lifestyle Design from a perspective of fun and imagination. There are no failures here, just play. Any challenges that arise are likely leading you to the necessary pivots that will inevitably lead to the life of your dreams. If you need support with this, consider working with me, and I can coach you through it.

For the Business Babes

Because you are queen and will inevitably get moving on building your empire, I want to encourage you not to do it alone. The one thing that has enabled me to maintain my desired lifestyle while growing my business is building a team that supports the movement.

We discussed this in earlier chapters, so I know you're good with it. But now I want you to think about support in a different way. For your business to support your desired lifestyle, you need to figure out what you're good at and what you suck at so that you can build a team to support your inevitable expansion. Pick people for your team who complement your skills.

What You Love

Gay Hendricks was first to come up with the "zone of genius" idea in his awesome book *The Big Leap: Conquer Your Hidden Fear and Take Life to the Next Level.*[64] Your zone of genius is where you are when you act on the unique, innate talent that makes you you. It's where you can capitalize on your natural abilities and skills in order to most easily fall into a state of flow. (*Flow* is psychologist Mihaly Csikszentmihalyi's word for when you're in the zone, doing something that totally absorbs your attention while feeling total happiness at the same time.)[65]

According to Hendricks, there are four states that people typically find themselves in:

- **Zone of incompetence:** You're not good at it, and many people can do it better.
- **Zone of competence:** You're average at it, and some people can do it better.
- **Zone of excellence:** You're highly skilled at it, and not many people can do it better.
- **Zone of genius:** You're exceptional at it, and no one can do it like you.[66]

As you might have guessed, not many people operate their lives from their zone of genius. Mostly because they (1) have no idea what their zone of genius is or (2) know what their zone of genius is but are too scared or embarrassed to rock it or (3) know what their zone of genius is but don't give themselves permission to request support to fill in the gaps in their skills because they feel they should do it all themselves.

If you fall into the first category, try answering these questions to help you identify your zone of genius:

Who were you in your youth? I'm talking about what kept you out past dark and had you rushing away from the dinner table so you could get back to it—your identity, your essence, who you were naturally without even trying.

When was the last time you felt really in the flow? Time didn't exist and hours passed without you noticing. What were you doing that had you so engaged?

What was the last great idea you had? Even if you didn't do anything with it, even if it was just a flicker of inspiration—what was it about?

When you think about times in your life and career when you felt the most fulfilled, can you see a central theme running through them? Your zone of genius might not be around a payable skill. Perhaps you've felt most fulfilled helping others in your neighborhood or coming up with innovative ideas for your family's lifestyle—you might not receive remuneration for this talent right now, but you love engaging in it nevertheless.

Now I don't expect you or any rational person to uncover your genius using just a few questions. I advise you to journal your answers and then think about them for a few days. Do some investigative research. Ask your parents what you were into when you were a kid. Read some old diaries. Reflect on your past gigs.

And once you do inevitably find your four different zones, and most especially your zone of genius, give yourself permission to act on this information. Personally, I am horrible at anything detail oriented or administrative—you'd be better off hiring a five-year-old, I'm that bad. This is my zone of incompetence. My zone of competence is sales. My zone of excellence is coaching one-on-one, and my zone of genius is presenting anything to a group, such as hosting my podcast, facilitating group coaching calls, and leading a group training.

Instead of beating myself up for being a horrible admin, I just rock my gifts and hire help to fill in my weaker spots—I don't have to do it all, or feel bad about what I'm bad at. This makes my business more fun, my message more effective, and my energy more focused on my purpose because I don't have to waste time trying to be something I am not.

As you're revolutionizing your life, keep your zones in mind and set up your lifestyle to take best advantage of your natural competencies. Remember that according to the Science of Happiness from Chapter 3, utilizing your strengths increases your happiness and makes you feel like it's a calling rather than just a job. So this is where your applying your strengths in your chosen vocation will feed into your level of happiness in your life. So put your strategy brain on, because this is what it looks like to be strategic about your life purpose. Now it's time to move on to the next design phase.

Your Desired Lifestyle

In my experience designing my lifestyle and helping clients design theirs, I've found that often we're so focused on finding our purpose that we forget to envision what living that purpose will look like on the daily. Before you start to go after your zone of genius, you must find a way to cultivate your genius in a way that works for you.

This requires some brainstorming and reflection. Maybe you've always wanted to travel the world, so you need to be a digital nomad with a fully remote career. Maybe you want to work ten hours a week, but you want to do so in a pet-friendly office surrounded by people you love. Maybe you want to afford a house in the mountains and fully retire by the age of thirty-two so you can live out your days woodcarving. Whatever the specifics, if you don't get clear on them now, they'll never happen. Here are a few questions to get you started.

- **In your ideal reality, how are you spending a typical day?** Get specific on how many hours you work, what activities you do, and who you're with.
- **How much money do you need to make a year to afford your ideal lifestyle?** GET SPECIFIC. If you want to live in a penthouse in NYC, google how much it costs to rent a penthouse in NYC. Whatever details you can think of—monthly yoga memberships, concerts every weekend, a closet full of Gucci—find the exact cost and add it all up.
- **What would be your ideal work scenario?** Hours, office, benefits, anything you can think of! A fun way to do this exercise is to create a description of your dream job or your dream role as the CEO of your lifestyle business.
- **What are three to five big goals in life that you will TOTALLY regret never achieving?** I'm talking about the things that you cannot die without experiencing first. Not smaller, society-induced objectives like "lose weight" or "make more money." I'm talking BIG things, like "step foot in every country," "write a book," or "star in a movie."

Your Bulletproof Why

This is one of the most important parts of Lifestyle Design. For a super sweetie such as you, I know you want to make a difference and help people. So, getting clear on how you will do this will fuel your fire and give your dream legs.

Before you put it all together, you need to figure out your why:
- What impact do you desire to make?
- What legacy do you want to leave?
- Whose life do you want to change?
- Why is this important to you?

As you know, I want to empower women, but when I get to the heart of my why, I shed tears of passion and desire to empower my daughter, Maya. I am not sure what the world will be like by the time she reads this book, but I am hoping it's a better and more equitable place. I want her to stand tall and feel important knowing that this book was dedicated to her. I want to leave her a legacy that she will feel empowered by. I want her to feel fully self-actualized. I want her to fly free in the face of imposed limitations and uncertainty. And more than anything, I want her to trust herself. I want her to have a high regard for the precious soul that she is, and I want her to express her soul's purpose to the fullest extent. I want her to soar.

This is the fundamental reason I do what I do. No challenge I will face will ever make me want that less, and for that reason my why is bulletproof.

Putting It All Together

By now you might have uncovered the fact that to be happy you somehow need to make a million dollars *and* work five hours a week. If you're deep in debt and working sixty plus hours a week, that dream lifestyle may feel next to impossible to attain.

Though it's fun to dream, it's more fun to dream in a way that's doable. Rather than focus on the big picture, I want you to begin by thinking about what little step you can take that will move you closer to that dream.

We must chunk it down into smaller, more easy-to-manage steps that, once achieved, will have you feeling enough momentum to keep going. So that one day you'll be waltzing across the finish line.

For example, say you realize you need to make $100K a year to afford your ideal lifestyle, and right now you make only $40K. That's a big jump, so why not chunk it down and make your next goal $50K or focus on monthly goals that grow bigger and bigger until, all of a sudden, the $10K addition isn't that far away?

If you're a little bummed that it's taken you this long to figure out your dream lifestyle, don't sweat it. Keep in mind that I started revolutionizing my life and became a coach only about twelve years ago. I became an entrepreneur and had the inspiration for this book eight years ago, and neither endeavor flourished until now. I had the dream to become a pilot four years ago, and only recently did I finally dip my toes in the industry; I probably won't actually fly a plane for another year or two.

The point here is this: There's no rush.

Just say yes to your desires, and put one foot in front of the other.

I have made the mistake of allowing social comparison to get to me. Comparing myself to entrepreneurs who have been in business as long as me but who are more monetarily successful. It feels bad, but I know that my path is my path, and their path is their path. Instead of feeling like where you are isn't enough, why don't you plant the seeds of your dreams, water them every day, and give them time to germinate?

Don't smother your seeds with the stress of a rigid timeline and social comparison. Just water your dreams daily and they will grow.

— Life Work —

Complete the exercises presented in this chapter. Grab a pen and your journal and let's get to creating that ideal lifestyle by your design.

1. Spend some time brainstorming your Revolutionary Life Formula.

2. Think through your zones of competence to get clarity on your strengths.

3. Think through the questions presented on your desired lifestyle.

4. Think about the impact you want to make and the legacy you want to leave.

5. What is your bulletproof why?

9

BE
the Revolution

Alone we can do so little; together we can do so much.
—Helen Keller

We've reached the final chapter in our journey together as women supporting one another. I hope my soul expressed through the pages of this book has served and inspired you.

If you've been implementing changes in your life and taking action along the way, I'm willing to bet that your life already looks different from when we first began. So much changes when you first change your mind.

And while you've taken massive leaps thus far, we're not even close to being done. You see, revolutionary is not a destination. It's a state of being. It's a feeling that you must return to every day in order to continue living life on your terms. Bucking the system, breaking the rules, and tuning in to the truth of your soul isn't easy in this crazy world.

It requires courage and leadership. It requires you to put yourself out there in ways you never have before, and if you're doing it right, you will trigger other people.

That's why this final chapter is all about what it takes to *continue* to be revolutionary at every stage of your life. Whether you're starting a business, looking for a partner, healing from past trauma, discovering your dharma, breaking generational curses, navigating an empty nest, or reinventing your entire life—you need courage.

We often think that courage is an internal trait, but it is actually external. It comes from the support we feel from others. When I finally left that toxic job, I was surrounded by a coach and a community who supported the wild idea that I could make that leap and still survive. Without their support I'd still be in dead-end jobs that underpay and undervalue me.

When I did stand-up comedy, I had a room full of people from the seminar I attended who were excited for me and couldn't wait to hear how it went when I finally went after my dream. It was their support that gave me courage to face my mother's disapproval. Without it I'd still be dreaming about the stage.

When I finally started my business, I was in a mastermind of women who were also entrepreneurs. Without them I might have never had the courage to start my business and build my brand.

There's a quote by Henry David Thoreau, "Most (wo)men lead quiet lives of desperation and go to the grave with the song still in them."

This quote breaks my heart because it rings so true. I don't want you to go to the grave with the song still in you. I want you to sing it. The likelihood of you singing it will be much higher if you have a tribe of abnormal, outlandish, revolutionary, atypical lady bosses by your side as you embark upon your revolutionary life. You need them to support you, encourage you, and remind you of who the fuck you are.

A Supportive Tribe

A queen runs an empire, but she doesn't do everything herself, right? If you want to live a revolutionary life, you need to be humble enough to ask for help. Vulnerable enough to admit that you need support. Realistic enough to realize that you are not going to get where you want to go if you keep walking alone.

And the idea of having support applies to all areas of our lives, not just our businesses. You can find ways to ask for help in your self-care by asking a friend to work out with you or hiring a personal trainer. You can ask your parents to babysit one night a week so that you can prioritize your need for a quiet evening or a date night.

There are a gazillion ways to go about finding help, but what's usually in the way is your mindset. If you're a recovering codependent like me, I imagine your mind floods you with thoughts like, "Is it okay to ask for help? Will I seem like too much? Do I sound needy? I don't want to be a burden. They probably have better things to do. I don't want to bother them."

These thoughts keep you suffering in silence and going it alone. So the most pressing help you should find is help to upgrade your mindset. I know you've made leaps and bounds by reading this book already, but true change doesn't happen in the mind, it happens in the body. So you need to take action and allow your nervous system to experience that it's safe to be supported. That will help you embark on the next chapter of your life in a revolutionary way.

I'm sure you've heard the Jim Rohn quote: "You are the average of the five people you spend the most time with." If that's true (and it is), who are the five people you spend the most time with? And are they contributing to your success, happiness, and fulfillment? Or are they holding you back? Undermining you and hoping you don't rock their boat?

I'm not saying you need to ditch all of your friends to be happy and successful, but I *am* saying that you need to actively seek positive, supportive relationships in your life that encourage you to shine and expand. Relationships that love you for who you truly are and honor your boundaries.

Finding a tribe of women who lift you up can be hard in this day and age. Many of my harshest wounds come from women I thought were my best friends getting triggered by my success and attacking me as a result. These attacks confirmed my belief that I needed to stay small in order to be in relationship with others. But that was just a reflection of where my mindset was at that time.

Now they don't confirm that at all. Now I see it for what it is, just another reflection of the toxic patriarchal matrix we were born into. It's in the ethers of our society, which means it can rear its ugly head in any form. It could be a mother, a father, a sister, or a brother. It could be your best friend, your cousin, your coworker, or your boss. It could be someone at church, a seminar, a colleague. It's the spirit of oppression and it can be in anyone, even you.

People often don't even realize when they're doing it, but we oppress ourselves and each other all the time. But what it means to be revolutionary is to revolt against any force that attempts to hold you down or hold you back from who you truly are and where your soul is meant to go.

The amount of joy, healing, support, and love I feel from healthy relationships with women who celebrate my shine has absolutely revolutionized my life. I now feel like it's safe to share my gifts with the world. I now feel like I am supported by a tribe of bad bitches who want to see me win. I now feel like I'll have someone to celebrate with when this book finally launches. And I also feel like I have a loving supportive tribe to process with when things don't go my way. I encourage you to unlearn, up-level, and cultivate a tribe so that you have support while you revolutionize your life.

Thank You

And, finally, I just want to tell you how proud I am of you. Take a look at all you've accomplished so far. The tough conversations, the crushed limiting beliefs, the goals you've dreamed up and gone after. It's all because *you* decided to make a change and disrupt a pattern that was holding you back. You are in control of your life, and you can design it however you like.

I take very seriously your commitment to growth and I treasure your willingness to allow me on this journey with you. Few connections are as sacred as that between a client and coach. The radical candor we share as you blow past small talk and share the desires of your heart is so special and soul-fulfilling to me.

I am honored to be in this vocation, and I thank you for supporting me in living out my ikigai. Because you have picked up this book, I know you are a truth seeker and that you are here for a purpose. It's been an honor to accompany you on your path, and I thank you from the bottom of my heart.

More than anything, I want you to walk away from reading this book with more power than you started with. More self-trust, more courage, and more belief in yourself.

In the movie *The Matrix*, right before Neo is about to choose the red pill, Morpheus gives him a speech.

> "The matrix is everywhere. It is all around us. Even now in this very moment, you can see it when you look out your window or when you turn on your television. You can feel it when you go to work, when you go to church, when you pay your taxes. It is the world that has been pulled over your eyes to blind you from the truth."

Neo asks, "What truth?"

You Are a Treasure

You are a divine soul with a purpose, and your purpose is of paramount importance.

You are inherently valuable.

You are more than how much money you make.

You are more than the current limitations in your life.

You are brilliant, beautiful, and wonderful.

You are precious, sacred, and special.

You are a treasure.

And you are also your treasure's keeper.

I pray that you keep yourself safe and raise your level of self-honoring to reflect what you truly deserve and desire.

I pray that you live a life that is worthy of your magnificent soul.

I pray that you revolt against any part of you that has bought into the spirit of oppression, subjugation, or the belief that you are less than.

I pray that you have an uprising within yourself that allows you to rest in the truth that you are more than enough.

I pray that the words in this book have permeated your spirit and that you are forever changed.

Changed into someone who truly believes in herself and her inherent value.

Who takes risks.

Who bets on herself.

Who listens to herself.

Who shines bright.

Who expands as she is inevitably meant to expand.

Who not only grows but also flourishes into the beautiful human you already were but had forgotten about.

I pray that this book has breathed more life into your life.

I see you. I honor you. I love you. And I am here for you.

Thank you for going on this journey with me and thank you for being a Revolutionary Woman.

ENDNOTES

Chapter 1

1. Tiffany O'Callaghan, "The Brain Science behind Why We Care What Others Think," Time, June 17, 2010, https://healthland.time.com/2010/06/17/the-brain-science-behind-why-we-care-what-others-think/. x

2. Kimberly A. Hamlin, "Women Asked for an Independence Day. They Got Mother's Day Instead," Washington Post, May 7, 2021, https://www.washingtonpost.com/outlook/2021/05/07/women-asked-an-independence-day-they-got-mothers-day-instead/.

3. Marcel Schwantes, "Study: The Workplace Is Now the Fifth Leading Cause of Death in the U.S. (Above Diabetes). Here Are the Top 10 Reasons Why," Inc., November 21, 2018, https://www.inc.com/marcel-schwantes/study-workplace-is-now-fifth-leading-cause-of-death-in-us-above-diabetes-here-are-top-10-reasons-why.html.

4. Susie Steiner, "Top Five Regrets of the Dying," The Guardian, February 1, 2012, https://www.theguardian.com/lifeandstyle/2012/feb/01/top-five-regrets-of-the-dying.

5. Suzanne McGee and Heidi Moore, "Women's Rights and Their Money: A Timeline from Cleopatra to Lilly Ledbetter," The Guardian, August 11, 2014, https://www.theguardian.com/money/us-money-blog/2014/aug/11/women-rights-money-timeline-history.

6. McGee and Moore, "Women's Rights and Their Money," https://www.theguardian.com/money/us-money-blog/2014/aug/11/women-rights-money-timeline-history.

7. History.com Editors, "Women's Suffrage," History.com, October 29, 2009, updated February 23, 2021, https://www.history.com/topics/womens-history/the-fight-for-womens-suffrage#section_6.

8   Tiffany Silverberg, "The History of Women and Money in the United States in Honor of Women's History Month," One Advisory Partners, March 7, 2017, https://www.oneadvisorypartners.com/blog/the-history-of-women-and-money-in-the-united-states-in-honor-of-womens-history-month.

9   McGee and Moore, "Women's Rights and Their Money," https://www.theguardian.com/money/us-money-blog/2014/aug/11/women-rights-money-timeline-history.

10 McGee and Moore, "Women's Rights and Their Money," https://www.theguardian.com/money/us-money-blog/2014/aug/11/women-rights-money-timeline-history.

11 McGee and Moore, "Women's Rights and Their Money," https://www.theguardian.com/money/us-money-blog/2014/aug/11/women-rights-money-timeline-history.

12 McGee and Moore, "Women's Rights and Their Money," https://www.theguardian.com/money/us-money-blog/2014/aug/11/women-rights-money-timeline-history.

13 McGee and Moore, "Women's Rights and Their Money," https://www.theguardian.com/money/us-money-blog/2014/aug/11/women-rights-money-timeline-history.

14 McGee and Moore, "Women's Rights and Their Money," https://www.theguardian.com/money/us-money-blog/2014/aug/11/women-rights-money-timeline-history.

15 McGee and Moore, "Women's Rights and Their Money," https://www.theguardian.com/money/us-money-blog/2014/aug/11/women-rights-money-timeline-history.

16 Tara Sophia Mohr, "Why Women Don't Apply for Jobs Unless They're 100% Qualified," Harvard Business Review, August 25, 2014, https://hbr.org/2014/08/why-women-dont-apply-for-jobs-unless-theyre-100-qualified.

17 Robin Bleiweis, "Quick Facts About the Gender Wage Gap," Center for American Progress, March 24, 2020, https://www.americanprogress.org/issues/women/reports/2020/03/24/482141/quick-facts-gender-wage-gap/.

18 "2020 Equal Pay Day Rally to Shed Light on the Experiences of Women of Color" [press release], Women Employed, March 31, 2020, https://womenemployed.org/press-release/2020-equal-pay-day-rally-to-shed-light-on-the-experiences-of-women-of-color/.

19 Aliya Hamid Rao, "Even Breadwinning Wives Don't Get Equality at Home," The Atlantic, May 12, 2019, https://www.theatlantic.com/family/archive/2019/05/breadwinning-wives-gender-inequality/589237/.

20 Lorie Konish, "Women Are More Likely to Leave Financial Planning to Their Spouses. Here's Why That's a Problem," CNBC, March 18, 2019, https://www.cnbc.com/2019/03/18/women-are-more-likely-to-leave-money-decisions-to-their-spouses.html.

21 Léa Rose Emery, "40 Percent of Households Are Now Headed by Women," Brides, October 24, 2019, https://www.brides.com/story/40-percent-of-households-are-now-headed-by-women.

22 Empowering Girls & Women, Clinton Global Initiative, https://www.un.org/en/ecosoc/phlntrpy/notes/clinton.pdf.

Chapter 2

23 "Merneith," Wikipedia, updated January 30, 2021, https://en.wikipedia.org/wiki/Merneith.

24 Patti Wigington, "The Egyptian Goddess Ma'at," Learn Religions, updated March 31, 2018, https://www.learnreligions.com/the-egyptian-goddess-maat-2561790.

25 Barbara Watterson, Women in Ancient Egypt (Stroud, United Kingdom: Amberley Publishing, 2013).

26 Joshua J. Mark, "Women's Work in Ancient Egypt," World History Encyclopedia, May 3, 2017, https://www.worldhistory.org/article/1058/womens-work-in-ancient-egypt/.

27 Much of the information in this section comes from: Joshua J. Mark, "Women in Ancient Egypt," World History Encyclopedia, November 4, 2016, https://www.worldhistory.org/article/623/women-in-ancient-egypt/.

28 "Neithhotep," Ancient Egypt Site, http://www.ancient-egypt.org/who-is-who/n/neithhotep.html.

29 J. Hill, "Female Pharaohs," Ancient Egypt Online, 2018, https://ancientegyptonline.co.uk/femalepharaoh/.

30 J. Hill, "Female Pharaohs," Ancient Egypt Online, 2018, https://ancientegyptonline.co.uk/femalepharaoh/.

31 Joshua J. Mark, "Women in Ancient Egypt," World History Encyclopedia, November 4, 2016, https://www.worldhistory.org/article/623/women-in-ancient-egypt/.

Chapter 3

32 Sonja Lyubomirsky, Laura King, and Ed Diener, "The Benefits of Frequent Positive Affect: Does Happiness Lead to Success?," Psychological Bulletin 131, no. 6 (2005): 803–855. https://www.apa.org/pubs/journals/releases/bul-1316803.pdf.

33 Belinda Luscombe, "Do We Need $75,000 a Year to Be Happy?" Time, September 6, 2010, http://content.time.com/time/magazine/article/0,9171,2019628,00.html.

34 Carol Nickerson, Norbert Schwarz, Ed Diener, and Daniel Kahneman, "Zeroing In on the Dark Side of the American Dream: A Closer Look at the Negative Consequences of the Goal for Financial Success," Psychological Science 14 (2003): 531–536. doi:10.1046/j.0956-7976.2003.psci_1461.x.

35 Dacher Keltner and Jason Marsh, "How Gratitude Beats Materialism," Greater Good Magazine, January 8, 2015, https://greatergood.berkeley.edu/article/item/materialism_gratitude_happiness.

36 Sarah E. Jackson, Andrew Steptoe, Rebecca J. Beeken, Mika Kivimaki, and Jane Wardle, "Psychological Changes Following Weight Loss in Overweight and Obese Adults: A Prospective Cohort Study," PLoS One, August 6, 2014, https://journals.plos.org/plosone/article?id=10.1371/journal.pone.0104552, cited in Tessa Berenson, "Losing Weight Could Make You Depressed, Study Says," Time, August 8, 2014, https://time.com/3092086/weight-loss-depression/.

37 Isak Ladegaard, "Mental Health Problems Worsen with Cosmetic Surgery," Science Norway, July 4, 2012, https://sciencenorway.no/cosmetics-forskningno-norway/mental-health-problems-worsen-with-cosmetic-surgery/1373674.

38 "Are Married People Happier than Unmarried People?" [press release], American Psychological Association, 2003, https://www.apa.org/news/press/releases/2003/03/married-happy; Richard E. Lucas, Andrew E. Clark, Yannis Georgellis, and Ed Diener, "Reexamining Adaptation and the Set Point Model of Happiness: Reactions to Changes in Marital Status," Journal of Personality and Social Psychology 84, no. 3 (2003): 527–539, https://static1.squarespace.com/static/54694fa6e4b0eaec4530f99d/t/54c7048ee4b0da34c29ca646/1422328974467/Reactions+to+change+in+marital+status+2002.pdf.

39 Ed Diener and Martin E. P. Seligman, "Very Happy People," Psychological Science, January 1, 2002, https://journals.sagepub.com/doi/10.1111/1467-9280.00415.

40 Diener and Seligman, "Very Happy People," https://journals.sagepub.com/doi/10.1111/1467-9280.00415; Ed Diener and Robert Biswas-Diener, "Will Money Increase Subjective Well-Being?" Social Indicators Research 57 (2002): 119–169, https://link.springer.com/article/10.1023/A:1014411319119.

41 Elizabeth M. Lawrence, Richard G. Rogers, and Tim Wadsworth, "Happiness and Longevity in the United States," Social Science and Medicine 145 (2015): 115–119, https://www.sciencedirect.com/science/article/abs/pii/S0277953615301222.

42 Sonja Lyubomirksy, The How of Happiness: A New Approach to Getting the Life You Want (New York: Penguin, 2008).

43 Brian J. Brim, "How a Focus on People's Strengths Increases Their Work Engagement," Gallup, May 2, 2019, https://www.gallup.com/workplace/242096/focus-people-strengths-increases-work-engagement.aspx.

44 Heather Craig, "The Research on Gratitude and Its Link with Love and Happiness," Positive Psychology, February 2, 2021, https://positivepsychology.com/gratitude-research/#gratitude-proven-benefits.

45 E. A. Vogel, J. P. Rose, L. R. Roberts, and K. Eckles, "Social Comparison, Social Media, and Self-Esteem," Psychology of Popular Media Culture 3, no. 4 (2014): 206–222, https://doi.apa.org/doiLanding?doi=10.1037%2Fppm0000047.

46 Nataly Kogan, "The Single Most Important Thing We Can Do for Our Happiness," Happier, https://www.happier.com/blog/how-to-find-happiness-the-single-most-important-thing-we-can-do/.

47 Stephanie Watson and Kristeen Cherney, "The Effects of Sleep Deprivation on Your Body," Healthline, medically reviewed by Stacy Sampson, May 15, 2020, https://www.healthline.com/health/sleep-deprivation/effects-on-body.

Chapter 4

48 Elizabeth Hopper, "Maslow's Hierarchy of Needs Explained," Thought Co., updated February 24, 2020, https://www.thoughtco.com/maslows-hierarchy-of-needs-4582571.

49 Kirsten Weir, "The Pain of Social Rejection," Monitor on Psychology 43, no. 4 (2012): 50, https://www.apa.org/monitor/2012/04/rejection.

50 Benjamin P. Chapman, Kevin Fiscella, Ichiro Kawachi, Paul Duberstein, and Peter Muennig, "Emotion Suppression and Mortality Risk over a 12-Year Follow-Up," Journal of Psychosomatic Research 75, no. 4 (October 2013): 381–385, https://www.sciencedirect.com/science/article/abs/pii/S0022399913003036.

51 Merav Knafo, "The Connection between Resentment and Cancer—and How to Stay Resentment-Free," The Vortex (blog), December 29, 2014, https://www.thevortex.me/resentment/; see also S. Greer and Tina Morris, "Psychological Attributes of Women Who Develop Breast Cancer: A Controlled Study," Journal of Psychosomatic Research 19, no. 2 (April 1975): 147–153, https://www.sciencedirect.com/science/article/abs/pii/0022399975900628 and S. P. Thomas, M. Groer, M. Davis, P. Droppleman, J. Mozingo, and M. Pierce, "Anger and Cancer: An Analysis of the Linkages," Cancer Nursing 23, no. 5 (2000): 344-349, https://pubmed.ncbi.nlm.nih.gov/11037954/.

Chapter 5

52 "Co-dependency," Mental Health America, https://www.mhanational.org/co-dependency.

53 "Co-dependency," Mental Health America, https://www.mhanational.org/co-dependency.

54 Cassandra Borges Bortolon, Luciana Signor, Taís de Campos Moreira, Luciana Rizzieri Figueiró, Mariana Canellas Benchaya, Cássio Andrade Machado, Maristela Ferigolo, and Helena Maria Tannhauser Barros, "Family Functioning and Health Issues Associated with Codependency in Families of Drug Users," Ciencia and Saude Coletiva 21, no. 1 (2016): 101–107, https://pubmed.ncbi.nlm.nih.gov/26816168/.

55 Betsey Backe, Erin L. Bonck, and Marie L. Riley, "Codependency and Depression: A Correlational Study," Journal of Couples Therapy 4, nos. 1–2 (1994): 105–127, https://www.tandfonline.com/doi/abs/10.1300/J036v04n01_08?journalCode=wzct20&.

Chapter 6

56 David Rock, "SCARF: A Brain-Based Model for Collaborating with and Influencing Others," NeuroLeadership Journal, no. 1 (2008): 1–9, https://qrisnetwork.org/sites/default/files/materials/SCARF%20A%20Brain-based%20Model%20for%20Collaborating%20with%20and%20Influencing%20Others.pdf.

57 "Marriage & Divorce," American Psychological Association, https://www.apa.org/topics/divorce-child-custody#:~:text=They%20are%20also%20good%20for,subsequent%20marriages%20is%20even%20higher.

58 Rock, "SCARF: A Brain-Based Model for Collaborating with and Influencing Others," 1–9, https://qrisnetwork.org/sites/default/files/materials/SCARF%20A%20Brain-based%20Model%20for%20Collaborating%20with%20and%20Influencing%20Others.pdf. Chapter 8

Chapter 7

59 Jessica Stillman, "Science Has Just Confirmed That If You're Not Outside Your Comfort Zone, You're Not Learning," Inc., August 14, 2018, https://www.inc.com/jessica-stillman/want-to-learn-faster-make-your-life-more-unpredictable.html.

60 Nico Bunzeck and Emrah Düzel, "Absolute Coding of Stimulus Novelty in the Human Substantia Nigra/VTA," Neuron 51, no. 3 (2006): 369–379, https://doi.org/10.1016/j.neuron.2006.06.021.

61 Kate Murphy, "Outsmarting Our Primitive Responses to Fear," New York Times, October 26, 2017, https://www.nytimes.com/2017/10/26/well/live/fear-anxiety-therapy.html.

Chapter 8

62 MABG Editorial Team, "Following Your Head vs. Your Heart," Medical Alert Buyers Guide, updated on August 23, 2020, https://www.medicalalertbuyersguide.org/articles/following-your-head-vs-your-heart/.

63 "The Right Outlook: How Finding Your Purpose Can Improve Your Life," Blue Zones, https://www.bluezones.com/2011/08/the-right-outlook-how-finding-your-purpose-can-improve-your-life/.

64 Gay Hendriks, The Big Leap: Conquer Your Hidden Fear and Take Life to the Next Level (New York: HarperCollins, 2009).

65 Mihaly Csikszentmihalyi, "Flow, the Secret to Happiness," TED Talk, video, 18:42, February 2004, https://www.ted.com/talks/mihaly_csikszentmihalyi_flow_the_secret_to_happiness.

66 Hendriks, The Big Leap.

ABOUT THE AUTHOR

*D*o you really need more info about me? I feel like I just told you all my dirty secrets, but sure why not.

Shereen Thor is a serial artist and entrepreneur who was finally able to bring all her talents and weirdness together when she built her brand and wrote this book. Born and raised in Los Angeles it all started when she rebelled against her immigrant mother's desire for her to become a doctor, lawyer, or engineer and instead became a comedian and coach.

She attended Temple City High School and grew up going to church at Pasadena Nazarene. She is a constant seeker of truth, connection, and adventure. She's a wife, and a mother of two. She would rather frolic freely than be bound by a schedule yet somehow she has found a way to function in society. She has been more obsessed with figuring out her life's purpose and living a meaningful life than making money and for that reason, she is forever grateful to you for buying this book. She really needs the money.

She knows she should be impressing you with all the bigtime media publications that have published her words, and all the executives she's coached at super cool companies. But she doesn't really care about that stuff because it's all based in ego, and she knows every human was created equal. She believes everyone has a unique purpose only they can fulfill. She doesn't want to waste time bragging because she doesn't want you fall prey to social comparison and diminish your inherent worth and value. The gift of life is so precious and she wants you to walk away from every interaction with her feeling more important and purpose-driven than when you started.

This book comprises everything she wishes she knew in her twenties that would have helped her grab her lady balls earlier on in life. It lays out the 9 steps of growth that were necessary for her to go from people-pleasing zombie to revolutionary woman, and she hopes that it absolutely revolutionizes your life too. She's not that into social media because she revolts against anything that compromises her well-being and happiness, so to connect with her, go to shereenthor.com.

Also, writing about herself in the third person is her jam.

www.ingramcontent.com/pod-product-compliance
Lightning Source LLC
Chambersburg PA
CBHW072158100526
44589CB00015B/2272